Blogging

5-IN-1 Bundle

The Complete Collection to Start Blogging for Earning $1000+ For Day in 100 Days with Ads & SEO

Advanced Online Marketing Strategies

1. *How to Start a Blog: The Best Approach to Start Your First Blog and Find Loyal Readers and Fans*

2. *How to Write a Blog: The Best Technique to Plan and Write Amazing Blog Posts for Growing Your Community 10X*

3. *Blogging for Profit: The #1 Beginner's Guide to Earn $100+ for Day in 30 Days (Only High-Profitable Online Marketing Strategies)*

4. *How to Make Money Blogging: The #1 Advanced Guide to Earn $250+ For Day in 90 Days with Search Engine Optimization Monetizable Techniques (Zero-Cost Online Marketing Strategy)*

5. *Blogging for Money*: The #1 Complete Guide to Earn $500+ For A Day in 100 Days with High-ROI Facebook Ads and Google AdWords Advertising

How to Start a Blog

The Best Approach to Start Your First Blog and Find Loyal Readers and Fans

Table of Contents

Mark Gray

Mark Gray is an online marketer expert in monetization with more than 10 years of experience in selling digital and physical high ticket products with blogs.

After his IT engineering degree, Mark started to work for one of the top 5 techs multinational company in the world. At the same time, he started to study the rules of marketing because he wanted to understand how a multinational company has become as it is.

He immediately understood the potentiality of applying the concepts of marketing but online.

After various years of mistakes, miss-understanding and loss of money, Mark finally quitted his highly paid job to focus himself in creating multiple sources of income.

Now he has several 6-figure online businesses and he finally decides to explain how he gained his results.

Introduction

The following chapters will discuss the basics of getting a blog up and going. While in theory, it may seem easy to start a blog, there's a lot that has to be put into it. The first thing you have to figure out is what platform you are going to pick for your blog.

The great thing is this book is here to help you solve those problems. We'll start by looking at different platforms to host your blog, and most of them are free. Then we'll move onto the tough stuff like picking the niche for your blog. This may or may not be something you have already thought about, but it is one of the most important things.

After that, we'll look at the best practices of writing blog posts. If you can't write good posts, how are you going to create any traffic for your blog? Next, you're going to want to know how to make friends with your competitors. They may be competition, but they can be of great value.

The remaining chapters will look at how to create a brand, generate traffic, why you need to keep a regular posting schedule, the importance of interacting with your readers, coming up with several posts at once, and integrating Facebook.

Successful blogs had a lot of time and effort put into them. They didn't become famous overnight. You've taken the right first step. You bought this book to learn how to make sure you create the best blog possible.

Picking a Blog Platform

Deciding that you are going to create a blog comes with a lot of choices and decisions. One of the first decisions is what platform are you going to use? There are a lot of different platforms out there, but we're going to take a look at the more common ones so that you can make the best choice.

Before you dive into this list, it will help if you know what type of platform you want. If you are a complete beginner, you will want to pick one that is easy to put together and won't require any coding skills. You will also want to think about the type of blog that you want to make.

When your blog starts to grow, you may end up changing how your site looks and you may want to add in more features. That means it will be important for you to pick a platform that has flexibility and can grow with you. If you start off with the wrong platform, it can be very difficult to switch later. Lastly, even if you haven't thought about making any money, it would be a smart idea to make sure that you will still have that option to do so later on.

WordPress.com

WordPress.com will store your blog content for free, but this also means that you will get a limited version of their software. It is still a great choice for people who use blogging as a hobby and who aren't interested in investing any money. It is also the perfect idea for people who will likely upgrade their blog to a self-hosted WordPress blog. WordPress also offers your first domain name for free, and the premium account is only $96 a year for hosting. You can get a business account, which gives you an online store, for $25 a month.

Pros:
- They have hundreds of themes to pick from.
- It's extremely easy. You don't need any design or coding knowledge.
- No costs for set-up.

Cons:
- A free site will come with a .wordpress in your domain.
- With a free blog, you don't technically own it, which means you don't have control over your ad revenue. WordPress also has the power to suspend your site whenever they want.
- It doesn't look as professional.
- Their functionality will be limited unless you get an upgrade.

WordPress.org

The software for this is free and it is about three dollars a month for hosting. When you have a self-hosted WordPress blog, it means that you use the WordPress software on a different server. By using this, you will have complete control over the website and make it look as professional as you want, edit your HTML code, and install plugins. Going this route is typically a good idea for a person who wants to invest a few dollars each month. This is best for business owners, bloggers that want to expand the functionality of their site, and professional brand builders.

Pros:
- There are search engine friendly options.
- You will have access to more than 20,000 free plugins and 1,500 free themes.
- It is user-friendly and you will have full customization options.

Cons:
- Since it is so popular, it is often vulnerable to security threats.
- When you host on a third-party server, it often requires you to have a bit of technical knowledge, but many hosts will offer great tech support.

Blogger

This is another free blogging service. It is owned by Google, which means you will have access to tools like Google Analytics, AdSense, and so on. However, Blogger is not at all as flexible as WordPress. This is a great platform for brand builders and hobby bloggers who aren't interested in investing in any type of money but may be interested in making a bit of money with ads. Since

Blogger is easy to use, it makes it a great platform for a beginner that is just learning.

Pros:
- You have access to the HTML code, so you will be able to customize it a bit.
- You can use AdSense ads.
- It is completely free and extremely easy to use.

Cons:
- You will have .blogspot in your title.
- You aren't able to self-host, so it is completely dependent on Blogger's offers.
- There aren't as many themes and not nearly as much storage as with WordPress.com.

Tumblr

Tumblr is a free and easy platform to use and it is very social. This is a great option for people who like to "reblog" posts. This is a good platform for microbloggers, so it is probably not the best place if you want to develop long-form content.

Pros:
- CSS and HTML access so that you customize it.
- Around 1,000 themes that you can choose.
- You have unlimited storage.

Cons:
- It can be quite hard to monetize.

- You are limited on plugins.
- Backing up the blog and bringing in content from different platforms can be hard.

TypePad

This platform costs $8.95 or more each month. TypePad is a great option for brand builders or business professionals who are okay with investing a bit of money each month. That price does bring you more features and a very professional site. However, a lot of people will tell business bloggers that they need to self-host a WordPress platform because it has a large community, but there are advantages to TypePad.

Pros:
- It is easy to use.
- You have unlimited storage.
- They host with their own servers, but you own the blog you create.

Cons:
- You are limited on customization.
- It will cost you a few dollars more each month than it does to self-host with WordPress.

Wix

This will cost you $4.08 or more each month. This is a great option for bloggers because it is ideal for businesses. It comes with e-commerce functions, and WIX makes creating your e-commerce website extremely simple, but the full control over the shop is going to be a bit limited.

Pros:
- They have hundreds of professional themes.
- You have up to 20 GB of storage.
- There are domain registration options.
- It is easy to use.
- You can integrate ads.
- You have unlimited bandwidth.

Cons:
- You are limited in customization.
- They don't have advanced e-commerce tools.
- They are more expensive than a WordPress blog.

They do have free options, and they are good ideas for hobby bloggers or novices who don't want to spend any money on their other paid options.

Medium

This site was started in 2012. Since then, Medium has grown into a large community of experts, journalists, bloggers, and writers. It is very easy to use platform with very limited social networking features.

Pros:

- You are able to focus only on your writing instead of having to design a website.
- It will allow you to reach existing communities of people that have similar interests.
- It is easy to use and it doesn't need any setup or coding skills.

Cons:
- You aren't able to run your own ads.
- Medium owns the audience, so if you lose your blog you will lose your followers.
- Your features are limited when it comes to building a brand or design.

Weebly

The paid options for Weebly begin at $8.00 a month and come with limited features. In order to unlock all of their features, you will have to pay around $49 each month. Weebly is a hosted platform that will allow you to come up with a website with drag and drop tools. It also comes along with dozens of themes that you will be able to customize with their web-based interface.

Pros:
- The free plan on Weebly will allow you to try them out before buying.
- Since Weebly hosts the site, it has a quick and easy setup.

- They have easy-to-use drag and drop features so you don't need any technical skills.

Cons:
- It's hard to export your Weebly site to a different platform.
- You have limited integration with third-party tools.
- They have limited built-in features, and you aren't able to add new features.

Deciding on what platform you want to use will depend on what you want it to be able to do.

Picking a Niche

This step could come before or after picking the platform for your blog. It might be better if you pick your niche first because you will have a better idea of what you need your platform to do. Either way, you have to come up with a niche.

Now, you may have an idea of what you want to write about, but you're not sure if it is going to work. Or, you may not have a clue as to what you want to write about. You're not alone. Picking out a niche is probably one of the hardest parts of beginning your blog.

There are likely a million different ideas jumping around in your head, or you could be struggling to even think of one thing. No matter where you roadblock is, this chapter is meant to help you find that perfect niche for your blog.

We're going to look at three questions that you will answer to help you figure out your niche that you will grow with, stick with, and you might monetize it later on. If, after that, you are still struggling, you'll even find some great blog ideas to get your creative juices flowing.

Why Do You Need a Niche?

The main idea of a blog would be to share your ideas and thoughts with other people, right? Then why can't you just write your ideas and thoughts down when they pop up?

There isn't any internet police that is going to break through your door if you don't stick to a single niche. And some people out there have found success with a scattered approach to their blog. But here's why that doesn't typically work for most.

Your readers won't always be interested in every single topic that you love. That means, unless you are able to turn yourself into the topic of your blog, it will be extremely difficult to come up with an audience.

Now, on the other hand, if you only pick a single topic, you will be guaranteed to find people that will be interested in one of the posts and will likely be interested in other posts as well.

Brainstorming a Niche When You're Stuck

That brings us back to needing a niche. Where can you find that niche?

Right now, all you need to do is brainstorm. Yeah, you will probably want to validate those ideas, but we'll get to that later. Try not to worry too much about the topics feasibility and try to create a long list of topics that you think you could blog about.

Instead of just gazing at a wall and running a bunch of ideas through your mind, let's look at a few good ways to come up with some ideas:

- Look at your house or room. Have a look around at the things that you own and see if any of them spark any ideas.

- Look at your daily life. This is the same idea. Think about the things that you do every day and see if you can think of anything.
- Think about the blogs you read.
- What magazine articles do you like?
- Have a look at your order history and popular products on shopping sites like Amazon and eBay.

Validate Your Brainstormed List

By now you should have a few ideas of things that you could write about. The next thing you need to do is to validate those ideas to figure out which one would be the best choice. Picking your best niche is a balancing act between these three things:
- Are you able to make money on this topic?
- Are other people passionate about this topic?
- How passionate are you about this topic?

Look at it this way. If you will:
- Choose a topic that you have a passion for that has products that you are able to sell to create an income, but there isn't anybody else out there interested, you won't ever earn any money or build an audience.
- You pick something that a lot of other people also like, but you aren't passionate about it, you will struggle to continue writing posts.
- You go with the topic that you love and that also has a really good audience, but there

aren't any money-making opportunities, then you could be popular, but you won't make any money. This could be okay if your goal isn't making money.

You are probably wondering how to pick a blog niche that meets all of the requirements. Answer the following questions honestly.

1. Are you going to love writing about your niche one year and 50+ posts from now?

   This is the biggest problem people will experience. There are loads of blogs out there where people will start off strong and post every single week for a month or so. However, they drop off all of a sudden. Soon it turns to just a single post each month. Then it slows down more. You then start to notice year-long gaps and promises of "post more often."

   This in no way is a negative judgment on those people. I'm just making a point that it can be hard to consistently blog about a topic. That means before you make a final decision, you have to do a bit of soul-searching to figure out if you are going to be happy writing about that topic. Think about these times:

   - Once the excitement of creating your blog has passed.
   - The moment a year has gone by.
   - Once you have come up with 50+ posts and you are having a hard time coming up with new ideas.

   Everything isn't all doom and gloom. There is going to be two things that will help you keep the steam going once that initial rush has passed.

- Everything will be a lot easier if you are passionate about your topic and you start to see success.
- You are always able to hire other writers or take guest posts if you run out of steam.

2. Are there any other people out there that want to read this topic?

Once you have made it through the first question, you will know that there is at least one person that is interested in a particular niche. You now have to figure out if there are other people out there who will want to join in on it. Thankfully, this question is a lot easier to find the answer to because there isn't as much soul-searching and just a lot of research.

How are you going to figure out if your niche has an audience?

Start by plugging your brainstormed niches into Google Trends. This is a free tool to use as well. This will allow you to find out two important pieces of information.

- If people are searching for your particular niche.
- If your niche receives decreasing or increasing interest.

This is by no means a deep analysis, but it is a pretty good place to start and it's easy to use. You can also compare your niche's popularity to other possible niches.

Next, you can do some keyword research. You should now have a rough idea of how popular your niche is from Google Trends. Since Trends uses relative numbers, it isn't necessarily the best guess of real numbers. This means it doesn't tell you how many people are searching for that particular item.

A keyword search will let you know how many people are searching for keywords associated with your niche each month. First, you need to write out a list of keywords that relate to your niche. If your niche was the keto diet, some good keywords would be keto diet menu, keto recipes, keto diet, and so on.

Take those keywords and then put them into a research tool like Moz Keyword Explorer and KWFinder. These will also suggest other keywords for you. There aren't any specific rules here, but you want the main search words to have around a thousand searches each month. If very few people are searching for your terms, it is going to be hard to create lots of blog posts that people will want to read.

3. Are you able to make any money?

By this point, if everything has gone well, you should have figured out:

- If you are going to be able to stick with the niche.
- If there are people out there who are going to be interested.

The last piece of the puzzle is figuring out if you will be able to make any money from it. If you are creative, there is a chance that you will make a little money from almost any niche, but only if you have an audience. Because of this fact, this question is the least important.

But no matter how much creativity you have, you can't skate past this fact:

Some niches will make more money than others.

How can you figure out if there is good money in your niche? More research! The first thing to do is to see how other blogs in your niche made their money. Open up some tabs with popular blogs that fit your niche. Search through them and see if they:

- Have banner ads or any type of advertisements.
- Write about different products with links so that people can buy them.
- Sell products they own.

This will give you a good idea of how well you can monetize your blog. Affiliate programs and Amazon are both great ways to make money with your blog. While ads may not be the best, it can still drive some revenue your way. Making your own product takes more creativity, but it can also be as simple as writing an eBook about your niche. It's important that the product is able to provide value to your followers.

Still Struggling?

Now, back at the beginning of the chapter, I promised I would provide you with some niche suggestions in case you were still struggling at the end of the chapter. I really hope that you have come up with your own niche at this point, though. But I know it can be quite difficult, and I promised I would help. Here are over 100 niche ideas for a blog. You still need to go through the steps above. Just because it's on this list, and it will likely have a big audience, doesn't mean you will be able to stick with it in the long run. You need to really enjoy what you write about.

- Television and Pop Culture
- Satire
- Poker
- Drawing
- Environmentalism
- Atheism
- Religion
- Gardening
- Career tips
- Drones
- Home Automation
- Tiny Homes
- Hiking
- Survivalism
- Learning a Language
- Local Business Marketing
- SEO
- Solar Power

- Off-The-Grid Living
- Mental Health
- Natural Medicine
- Specific Medical Conditions
- Massage
- Landscaping
- Interior Design
- Retirement
- eSports
- Video Games
- Home Brewing
- Liquor
- Wine
- Beer
- Writing
- Meditation
- Public Speaking
- Standing Desks
- Productivity
- Self-Improvement
- Learning an Instrument
- Music
- Divorce
- Marriage
- Dating
- Movies
- Pregnancy
- Homeschooling
- College Applications
- Career Advice
- Motorcycles
- Cars

- Real Estate
- Cryptocurrency
- Investing
- Baking
- Specific Diets
- Recipes
- Cooking Tips
- Parenting
- Personal Style
- Makeup
- Acne and Skincare
- Uber or Lyft tips
- Airbnb Tips
- Couponing
- Frugality and Budgeting
- Graphic Design
- Coding and Development
- YouTube
- Education
- Pets
- Home Improvement
- Arts and Crafts
- Sewing and Knitting
- DIY Projects
- Funny Workplace Stories
- Mobile App Development
- Boating
- Fishing
- Minimalism
- Self-Publishing
- Freelancing
- Fashion

- Living Abroad
- Social Media
- E-Commerce
- Shopify
- WordPress
- Photography
- #vanlife
- RVing
- Location Independence and Digital Nomadism
- Your Local Area
- Running and Marathons
- Ironman or Triathlons
- Yoga
- Bodyweight Fitness
- Weightlifting
- Travel Hacks
- Travel
- Financial Independence
- Physical Sports
- Personal Finance

Writing Posts

You've made it through picking a platform and you have chosen your niche, now it's time to get down to business. You have to start writing your blog posts now. You need to write posts that people will enjoy reading and leave them wanting to come back.

This chapter will teach you tips/guides for your blog which you can adhere to when writing your posts. We're also going to look at the five main types of blog posts:

1. The Newsjacking Post
2. The SlideShare Presentation Post
3. The Curated Collection Post
4. The List-Based Post
5. The How-To Post

Nowadays, provided that you have a working knowledge and understand what you want to write about, you can now easily create a blog about it. If you are an expert in your chosen niche, there shouldn't be any reason for you to not hammer out some excellent blog posts.

Understand Your Audience

Before you write down a single word, it is imperative that you clearly understood the wants and needs of your blog viewers. What do they want to learn from your posts? Will it have an impact on them? For example, if your niche is business, and you know most of your readers are millennials, they aren't going to want to read about getting started with social media. The majority of them already have that down pat.

You could, however, provide them with information about how to switch up their social media approach from casual to a business-savvy approach. This small tweak is exactly what separates a person from blogging about generic things to blogging about what the audience is really going to want to read about.

Blog's Theme

Part of engaging readers is to make sure that they actually find and stay on your site long enough to read your blog. The first step to that is picking out a good domain name. This is important, but it's not something you need to stress over. Something as simple as using your first and last name will work. If you already have a business, you could use your business name. The important thing is that it makes sense for your niche.

The next thing is to make sure that you set up your blog in an effective manner. The appearance of your blog is very important to your readers. If you write about eco-friendly products, the color green could be a good idea. The first two things you need to make sure you need to do is add your logo and the about me page.

The logo can be your name or the logo of your business. Either way, it will help to remind your readers about whom and what they are reading.

How heavily you end up branding your blog is up to you.

The about me page is a blurb about you or your own business. This is an extension of you. Think about what you want to achieve with your blog. Maybe knowing about your background will help your readers or whatever will help drive your blog.

Picking Your First Post Topic

Before you start to write out any post, you are going to have to decide on a topic. To start out, you can try out the usual or common ones i.e. if you write a plumbing blog, you could make an intro with writing about leaky faucets. With more research, you could develop it further to talk about steps on solving their dilemma with leaking faucets basing on what happened prior to the problem.

It's probably a good idea to not jump right into "how-to" articles when you first start out posting. Maybe you would prefer writing about modern faucet setups, or share your experience with successfully repairing it thereby preventing the flood that might have happened in your house.

Sticking with the plumber example, if your first thought is to write a how-to post on fixing a leaky faucet, the following would be four other options to write about first:

1. News Post – a new study has found that X% of people don't replace their faucet when they should.

2. SlideShare Presentation – five different faucet types that need to replace your old one. This one should have pictures.
3. Curated Collection Post – ten faucet and sink brands that you need to look at.
4. List-Based Post – five ways to solve your leaky faucet problem.

A good idea is to look through your keyword list from the niche chapter. That could give you some good ideas for a first post. There are a few things you can do with a single topic to turn it into several different posts:

- Bring up some new formats.
- Taking a negative or positive approach.
- Picking a different audience.
- Changing up the time frame.
- Switching up the topic scope.

Create a Working Title

This will likely come up during the previous step. There will be different titles depending on how you want to approach your post. With the plumber example, you may choose to narrow the topic to "Tools to Fix a Leaky Faucet" or "Common Causes of Faucet Leaks." Your working title will help guide your post so that you are able to begin your writing.

Take this title for example: "How to Create a Viral Blog Post." It's a pretty good title, right? The topic for this post would probably be blogging. The working title could have been "The Process of Coming up with a Viral Post." And then they ended up titling their post "How to Create a Viral Blog Post."

Notice how it flowed starting at a subject on hand to a workable title and then the final name for your post. Your working title may not end up being your final title; however, it will still give you enough information in order for you to focus your post on specific aspects and not generalities.

Create a Captivating Intro

The first thing a reader is going to read is what? It's the introduction. You want the introduction to be captivating. First of all, it needs to grab their attention. If you end up losing their attention in the first few sentences, they aren't going to finish your post even if it is good information. There are several ways to grab their attention: grip them with a statistic or fact, be empathetic, or tell a joke or a story.

Then you will want to make known the intention of your post sharing to them the ways it will help them solve their issues. This is going to give them the motivation to continue looking over your posts and also help establish a kinship with the blog visitors. They will also know that your post is going to improve their life or work.

Organize the Content

Some blog posts will have a lot of information for the reader and the writer. To solve this problem, you have to organize the information in order for the readers not to feel intimidated by the amount of content. You can organize your content in many different ways such as tips, lists, sections, or whatever works for your post. The important thing is to make sure that it is organized.

To finish up, you will have to create an outline for your topic. This will help in figuring out all the points that you want to cover in your post.

Write Your Post

The next to do is to write your actual post, but it is not the last. Once you have your outline, you can now fill in all of the blanks. You should use your outline as a guide and make sure that you are ready to expand on any of the points that you need to. Write about the things that you already know, and if you need to, do some research to come up with more information, data, and examples. Make sure, if you incorporate external sources, that you provide proper attribution. If you are having a hard time finding compelling and accurate data for your post, you can try some roundup sources like Google Trends or Pew Research.

If you discover that you are having a hard time stringing those sentences together, you're not alone. A lot of people have a hard time finding their "flow." Luckily, there are a lot of tools out there that can help you to improve your writing skills. You can try websites like Cliché Finder, ZenPen, and Power Thesaurus to help you out.

Edit, Proofread, and Format

Just because you have written your post doesn't mean you are done, but you are closer. The editing process is one of the most important parts about your blogging work, and it should never be overlooked. If you have somebody that you can trust to proofread your post, you can ask them to read over it to see how it flows. You can also use free grammar software like Grammarly. The first thing you should do, though, is to read it through as soon as you get done.

The next important thing in the editing process is to pick a visually appealing and relevant image for the post. Since social media treats content with images in a better manner, visuals play a big part in the success of your blog. In fact, it has been found that content that has relevant images will receive 94% more views than those without images.

There are a lot of free stock image websites out there to find that perfect photo.

Visual Appearance

Nobody is going to want to read an ugly blog. And this doesn't mean only pictures; it's also organization and formatting. When a blog post is properly formatted and is visually appealing, you will find that sub-headers and headers are used to separate large text blocks, and all of those headers should be styled consistently.

If you use screenshots, they also need to have similar and defined borders in order for them to appear natural and not like they are floating in space. Your style also needs to stay consistent in all of your posts. Keeping up with your consistency will make your content and brand look a lot more professional, and it will make it easier on the eyes.

Tags and Topics

Tags are the specific keywords that describe your post. They will allow your readers to browse for more content in those categories on the blog. Keep away from adding in a laundry list of tags for every post. Instead, you should put some thought into your tagging. Tags should be viewed as categories or topics, and you should pick ten to 20 tags that represent your main idea.

Call to Action

At the end of your blog post, you need to add in a CTA that indicates what it is that you want your readers to do now. This could be subscribing to your blog, getting your book, registering for an event or webinar, read something related, and so on. Typically, the CTA should be beneficial for the marketer. A visitor will read your post, click on your CTA, and you will eventually make a lead. But this is also a great resource for your reader. You should use your CTAs to offer your readers more content on similar topics.

Optimize for SEO

Once you have finished writing, you need to optimize the post for search engines. You shouldn't obsess over the number of keywords that are included. If you have opportunities to incorporate keywords and it won't affect the reader's experience, go for it. If you are able to make the URL shorter and keyword friendly, do it. But you shouldn't cream keywords just for density. You should look at these aspects:

- Meta Description – these are the descriptions that appear just below the title on Google's search results. They will provide searchers with a summary of the post before they click on it. They should be around 155 characters and begin with a verb like discover, learn, or read. These descriptions no longer factor into Google's ranking algorithm, still, they do give readers a snapshot of what they will find in your post and can help with your click-through rate.

- Title and Headers – most platforms will use your post title as the page title, which is one of the most important SEO elements. But with this formula, you should already have a title that is naturally full of keywords and phrases. Do not make things complicated. Use keywords that are necessary and keep it simple. Your headlines should be kept short, less than 65 characters. This keeps search engines from chopping them off.

- Anchor Text – these are what connect your post to other pages. Make sure you pick these carefully because search engines take these into consideration when they rank your page.

Choose Your Final Title

This is your last step. You need to spruce up your working title. Consider these things:

1. Begin with your working title.
2. When you are editing your title, remember the importance of keeping it clear and accurate.
3. Sexy is the way to go. In this, choose a strong language, words that rhyme, and other creative and unique techniques.
4. Try to throw in keywords that enhance it for the SEO but it should be natural.
5. Finally, figure out if you can shorten it. Nobody enjoys long titles, and Google prefers less than 65 characters.

Now you know how to come up with an amazing post that people will want to read.

Turning Competitors into Friends

Blogging shouldn't be something you do alone. If you do, you'll find it extremely hard to bring in readers. It's not impossible, but if you have friends in your niche that are already established, it will be a lot easier. You need to know how to build relationships with other people.

Why do you need to make friends with other bloggers?

Here are a few great reasons to convince you to create solid friendships with other bloggers:

- You can't blog alone. I'm sure you're not interested in creating a ghost town blog. You are going to want to feel as if your blog matters. You want to see others interacting with you.

- It's important that you stay inspired. You need to draw inspiration and energy from your buddies in order to stay consistent in the things that you do. Plus, it is a good idea to stay motivated in order to continue writing great posts because you know people are going to read your posts. Isn't it better and more fun to do things with friends?

- You will have each other's back. When you connect with other bloggers within your niche, it will definitely be an effective way to ramp up marketing. It works a lot like, you scratch their back, and they scratch yours. You need to create a solid tribe where you want to do whatever it takes to help each other out.

It works out as a win-win for everybody. You will have some fun with all of your blogging buddies while you also work to build your traffic and connections. Let's look through some different ways to build lasting online blogging friendships, and how to find them.

1. Know when to jump in.

Friendships work the same online as they do offline. In order to create a relationship, you have to inject yourself into their world. It is actually easier than it sounds. All you have to do is start a conversation. Don't over think things. Pay close attention to the conversations they have with others online and figure out a way to join in naturally.

Familiarize yourself with their content and brand and understand their audience. Do some research and look through their social media. Read their blogs and bios, and make all of your comments count. Share their work with your network, and make sure that you tag them so that they know you are sharing their work.

If you really want to impress them, write a post with good content about them. This is where you can shine a light on their work. This is a great way to build a relationship with people that you want to make a connection with. To find these bloggers, head to an authority site within your niche and figure out the blogs that these sites link to.

2. Shadow popular bloggers.

What counts more are the people that you know not so much what you know. A good way to start building relationships is to shadow those who have popular blogs in your niche. Come up with a list of ten to 20 popular bloggers. Shadow them by staying up to date on their posts, follow them on social media, and comment on their blogs for around three weeks. This will make sure that you show up on their radar. Once you have done that, you can email them a pitch for a guest blog post or ask a question for a roundup post.

NinjaOutreach is another great tool to find bloggers in your niche. They even have a Chrome extension.

3. Show some love.

Blogging is a very creative endeavor, no matter the subject. Creativity wants to be fostered, enjoyed, and shared. That being said, you need to show other bloggers some love. Comments and shares are great options if you believe that you can add value. Another great way to find blogs is to use Google. You can also find them on social media sites as well.

4. Get in touch with them so that they know you appreciate their work.

You will have to take the plunge and direct message them at some point. This could be on Pinterest, Twitter, or you could shoot them an email. Let them know that you appreciate their work. This will help you to get on their radar and come up with some trust.

You can also join some Facebook groups surrounding your niche to help you find some people to make connections with. Pinterest is also a great social media site to make connections on.

5. It's not about you; it's about your readers.

No matter how much you want to believe that you can be successful with your blog, you aren't going to be able to do it alone. You have to have people. You also can't approach this with the thought that it is all about you because you would be wrong. It should focus on how you can help your readers with their issues.

You have to be open to responding to people if they were to have a question. You should also be able to elaborate more in your comment. If you are able to help them, then they will become a fan. Reach out and start a conversation even if you only say hello. Think about it like this. You like what that person writes about and you would like to know more about them. It won't take that much work to open a door in order to create a good relationship. When a person comments on your blog, look to see if they have one of their own and if it is in your niche.

6. Take the time and be consistent.

While in theory making connections are easy, it can still prove to be quite difficult for some more than others. It's even harder when you try to create a relationship with bloggers that have a large influence already. They already are plagued with a lot of people who are trying to "build relationships" with them. This means that there are quite a few different ways you will have to approach them.

Making connections can be time-consuming and work more like a process. With each step, you will become more personal, and it will take a little more time to make it through each stage.

Step 1 – Begin with social media, just like in the other tips. Figure out which sites that they are more active on and start liking and retweeting what they share. Start to pay attention to their engagement. If you start to get likes and favorites back, then you know your effort is working because they are noticing you. After a little bit, go beyond the norm and try doing something that gets you noticed such as making a graphic with one of their quotes.

Step 2 – Start leaving comments on their blogs because bloggers will respond to comments. Leave helpful comments in order to start a conversation. The first two steps are about becoming more visible to the person.

Step 3 – This is the biggie. Reach out through email. Commenting on their blogs is great and all, but it's more of a group discussion. With an email, you can get deep because it is only between you and the blogger. This is how you can grow your relationships.

Step one can be used as often as you want. Step two should be done only if it makes sense. With step three, you need to use this the least often. Once you start to build a bond, you will start to figure out which method you should use and how often. There are some people out there that are more receptive and creating a relationship with them will go faster and easier. On the other hand, there are going to be some that you can't connect with no matter how hard you try. The longer and more consistent approach normally works the best.

Now you should have a good idea on how you can make connections with other bloggers, and why it is so important.

Building a Visual Brand

How can you stand apart from your competitors? How can you create a brand identity that tells your story without saying anything? Why is it important to use visual branding?

There's a bunch of misleading and confusing information out there about branding. Let's figure it out.

Brand identity is the way an audience sees you. You need to look at your brand as a person. Let's try another step and look at it as a friend of your audience. Instead of looking at the audience as a faceless and nameless crowd; focus on one person or idea that you are befriending or targeting with your brand.

For you to make friends with a person, you have to influence the way they see you. This person will constantly be your friend when you share their values, are consistent, and enrich their lives.

Visual branding is the way you show others the friend you will be. You need to use it to influence the way your audience sees you.

If someone looks at your Instagram posts, and see it full of fun photos around your office, it might tell others that the happiness of your employees is important. If they see images of nature along with inspiring quotes, they might think you value motivation and encouragement.

You need to use visual clues in order to give those abstract ideas.

You might be playful, fancy, acerbic, irreverent, feminine, and authoritative. A visual will show those things quickly.

When people visit your website, the colors you chose, the text size, and the mood of your design will show them exactly how they need to feel about your brand.

This is the main reason visual branding is important. It doesn't matter whether or not you are knowingly influencing your audience; they are defining your brand. If what they see doesn't match your values, it is going to alienate, confuse, and disappoint the audience.

Visual brand identity is a lot more than pictures. It is everything your audience sees when they see your post. All of these elements will tell your story. This story will either reaffirm your values or completely take away from them.

Building your visual brand identity is fairly easy to accomplish. Let's look at some ways to influence the way your audience sees your brand. After you have answered these questions, you will be able to understand your visual brand identity.

How Do You See Your Personality?

After you know your audience and what you are offering them, the challenge now is the "how." How can you visually present your personality? With online blogs, many people face the challenge of expressing their personality without being able to interact with them face to face. When your sales team or customer service people put a face with your brand, online blogs create barriers.

The barrier gets steeper when you plan to use just text to bring in an audience.

We all love to text, but when you are promoting and building your brand identity, there is a lot more to it than just writing down some words. Using visual references will help you add tone along with your words.

Think about ways you can use images on your site to show key points about your personality.

Finding Emotion

A great way to reach an audience is with emotions. Is your brand telling a story that is going to move your customers?

Think about commercials you've seen about the exercise program P90X. It stirs emotions in their customers. They target couch potatoes but show you what is possible when you get up off that couch and begin exercising. You will be transformed into a muscle bursting and fat burning machine in just 90 days. Did it get you pumped? Were you ready to stop eating potato chips and make a new you instead of just watching it pass you by? This is the emotion that is behind this brand.

Should You Keep It Simple?

Visual brands don't need to be complicated. If you have too much going on, you are risking confusing your audience. This might seem a bit much. Get rid of everything that doesn't contribute to your brand.

Keeping It Consistent

Laura Bezant, the Jeweler, has a very distinct style with her brand. When you visit her Instagram account, you will see images all in similar tones. These are sun-washed images that all have the same color story.

Consistency lies in using the same filter, same size, and same font across all the visual platforms. It creates unity, so if someone follows you on Facebook and not Instagram, they are going to get the same story on either website.

Easily Understood?

Your story doesn't need to be so obscure that you have to brainwash your audience so they understand your message. If someone stumbles onto your site, will they understand what you are offering? Your visual branding needs to make sense along with your identity.

Can You Speak the Language?

You need to be fluent in the social media conversation. When you are working on your visual branding, it is the key to finding the right content to use on every platform for that particular audience. Pinterest offers helpful tricks and tips, DIY advice, and recipes. If you post images on Pinterest, they need to be in action with your audience. You want them to "pin" it to increase exposure. You also want them to continue onto your site.

Google Plus and Facebook are about community. These platforms are used for conversations with your audience. Use it to get interests to develop your brand.

With Twitter, you only use shorts comments, catchy imagery, and shameless self-promotion. Instagram shows small slices of your life.

Do You Brand on Social Media?

Take opportunities to become human with your customers, followers, and friends on social media. You have to use every inch of real estate to perfect this.

Creating cover images for boards on Pinterest will make it easier to get your audience engaged with you. This goes along with being consistent.

Do Logos Confuse You?

You aren't a logo. Logos are great to have since it has its own intrinsic meaning. While developing your brand identity, your audience will eventually associate your brand as your logo. They will then transfer all these perceptions onto your logo.

This isn't saying you don't need to worry about your logo. But just keep it simple; let the colors meld with your branding message.

Correct Font?

Words might not be used with visual branding, but typography is. Fonts can convey your tone. People can learn a lot about your brand just by the font you choose.

What Colors to Use?

When you are visual branding, using color is everything. There is a psychological attachment to every color. For example:

- Blue conveys calm, loyalty, and trust.
- Purple conveys original, creative, and luxury.
- Red conveys excitement, passion, and urgent.
- Green conveys natural, growth, and fresh.
- Black conveys refined, classic, and power.

You should just use two colors for maximum visibility of your stationery, website, and logo. When you use photos on social media, they are going to have more than two colors on them. You can create consistency if you use the same filters on every photo. Find the right color scheme that harmonizes with your brand.

Generating Traffic

The largest source to get traffic to your blog is going to be search engines. More than likely it will be Google. You could boost traffic to your blog that comes from search engines by applying SEO tricks into your writing and layout. You can easily start with just some general keyword research and figuring out what keywords will drive more traffic your way. When you have a list, try to incorporate these words into your blogs by using these tricks.

Put Keywords in the Title of Your Post

The easiest and best way to use keywords in your posts is to put them in the titles. Your title might have the ability to motivate people to click through on its own. If it's a strong title, leave it alone. Otherwise, try incorporating keywords into it if possible.

Use a Few Keywords or Phrases in the Post

Try to focus on optimizing your posts by using a few keywords or phrases in each of them. This will maximize how much traffic comes your way. Using too many keywords will dilute the content of your blog. It might look like spam to search engines and your readers.

Use the Keywords Through the Entire Post

If you can use the keywords throughout the entire post multiple times, without stuffing too many in there, it can boost your SEO. Try to use the keywords within the first few words of your blog, many times throughout, and at the end of the post.

Use the Keywords Around and in the Links

Experts think the search engines put more weight on the text that is linked when they rank results. It is best to include the keywords next to or in the links in your blog when it is relevant for you to do.

Utilize Keywords in Image Alt-Tags

You can choose to add alternate text for images you upload to your blog. This appears if visitors can't see or load an image in their browsers. This alternate text could help with SEO efforts. This is because the alternate text will appear in the HTML of your post content as an alt-tag. Search engines including Google use that tag to provide results for any keyword searches. Take some time and add any keywords that are relevant to your image and then post the alt-tag for every image you have uploaded and published to your blog.

Keeping a Regular Schedule

Blogging is fun for a lot of people. If you love blogging, you need to create a schedule to help you stay on track. Here are some tips and techniques to create and keep a constant schedule.

Think About This First

The biggest secret behind successful blogging is being consistent. It is similar to exercising; it is hard to get started. After you have gained some momentum, it isn't all that difficult to keep going. If you completely stop, you are going to find it hard to begin again. This is the main reason you need to make staying consistent top priority.

If you have to keep an aggressive schedule, you need to set time limits for every post.

Find an Inspiring Planner

DO NOT skip this. You can't keep things in your brain. You will not have good results.

Find a planner that speaks to you. If you love cats, find one that has cats on it. Flowers, star wars, dogs, nature, waterfalls, you get the picture. Carry it everywhere you go to keep you inspired. You can use whatever you like to check off all your daily goals. You could also choose to use a digital system, app, or find one online.

Figure out the Numbers

You need to know how many blogs you want to publish in the entire year. Whatever number you come up with, divide that by 12. This will tell you how many posts you need to write every month in order to reach your goal. Is your number reasonable? Do you feel inspired? Is it going to push you but not completely break you? Do you feel excited to begin working toward your goal?

Will you be able to write that many blogs without sacrificing the quality of your work? Sit down with a calculator, pen, and paper. Play around with the numbers. Work them until you have it down to a weekly or monthly goal that makes you feel good. Now, you can begin scheduling.

Make Your Weekly Schedule

You know how many posts you have to write every week, now you have a place to begin. Jot down that number. It might be one, three, or even more every week.

Pick a day every week to plan the next week's schedule. Make sure to take into account the number of posts you need to write that coming week.

Whatever number you have to write each week, document them in your planner, and check them off as you get them written. Schedule in the time you need to actually do your scheduling. It is another activity you have to take into consideration.

It is best to just make a schedule for one week mainly because most people don't know that far in advance what is going to be taking place. This week you might be able to write two posts on

Wednesday, but next Wednesday, your child has a play a school you are going to go see.

By making your schedule ahead of time, you will fit your blogging into an existing schedule with ease and flexibility. This is the main ingredient for reaching your goals and keeping your schedule.

If your week is super busy and you don't have time for any blogging, you will have to write double the next week to make your monthly goal. You might be able to fit a few posts into your plans somewhere in the week. By doing this, if something happens unexpectedly, you will still be able to meet your goals.

Some Advanced Strategies

After you have gotten used to your schedule, you could begin adding in a few more strategies. These might include creating a list of your SEO keywords, scheduling more posts, and blogging in batches.

Another strategy is training your brain to blog topics daily as you go about your normal routine. Jot these ideas now immediately. You may have noticed that certain bloggers never seem to run out of things to blog about. This is because they have learned how to do this technique. When you've gotten the hang of it, you won't ever run out of ideas.

You have to figure out what will work best for you. You can't use another person's schedule or ideas. They have to work for you or you won't have any success.

Get Advice from Your Readers

In order to have a successful blog, you will have to constantly create content that is informative and add value. You need to have an audience or tribe of readers who engage with your blog and follow you regularly. These people will read your blog posts actively and will subscribe to mailing lists in order to get updates when you put out new posts.

They always read and comment when you publish new posts, and always come back for more. These loyal participants will even advertise your blog to people who follow them both online and offline.

The hard part is building active readership and connecting to them better. Let's look at some tips that will help you connect better with your audience.

Respond to Comments

You need to respond to comments that people leave on your social media and blog posts. This is the best way to get your visibility out there and prove that you are an authority on certain subjects. When a reader leaves you a comment, do you take the time to respond to them?

If not, you are losing readers. It doesn't matter how busy you are, take time to respond to comments.

Just because you respond to a comment doesn't mean it ends there. You still have to engage your readers by email and on social media. Many might leave a comment or ask you a question about an issue or content.

Others might contact you by email to find an answer to their problem. You need to answer their questions and respond to comments on social media and blog posts.

Speak Directly

You should develop a strong brand image and a brand voice. A brand voice is what you put into your content that speaks to your audience. Why should you use social media along with your blogs? This is where your target market comes to communicate with you.

They may have feedback or questions about a blog post, a service, or product. You have to speak with your brand voice. This is the only language they will understand. Be sure you aren't speaking to everyone at one time because everyone is at a different stage in their journey.

When you are creating content for social media or a blog post, you have to put yourself in their shoes. Try to think as your ideal buyer or customer might think, and create content that they can connect with.

What question did they ask?
What did they suggest?
What was their opinion?

You need to always think about your ideal readers and write for them. Offer them what they are looking for.

Using the word "you" in your content will give your audience an understanding of the messages you are putting out there. "You" is a very powerful word in the English language. It will help you speak better to your audience.

You might be speaking to one particular person but your message will appeal to everyone.

Use Metaphors

You can use metaphors to connect with your audience better. Why metaphors? Using metaphors connects you with your audience because they explain hidden concepts in simple ways. They also help make hard subjects easier to understand.

What's a metaphor?

A metaphor is a way to speak that refers to something by mentioning a different one to create the rhetorical effect. It might give clarity or help see similarities of two ideas.

By using metaphors in your posts, it will make your content very clear. Your audience will be able to relate and it will be more engaging to them.

In order to impact your readers better and connect with them, be more specific when you use metaphors.

Your posts will:
- Be more engaging.
- Attract more readers.

- Be more persuasive.

Add Humor and Emotion

Most people underestimate how powerful humor and emotion is. Many people don't realize that when they read a blog post or book, and it makes them cry, laugh, or smile, they are experiencing humor and emotion. Being emotional can move you to tears of joy or make you smile.

This is just human nature and everybody can relate to it. When words can spark emotions in somebody, it will set off chain reactions that won't be replicated. It might be sorrow, happiness, or anger. Emotions are a powerful way you can connect with your audience.

When you are creating your blog, find opportunities to add in some humor or emotion that will align with others. You might tell your life story, or other experiences your audience might be able to relate to. You might just be able to help them solve a problem they might be having.

Content like that can connect you to your audience a lot better.

You have to build relationships to connect with others and grow your audience. You have to understand the best ways to help you connect with them better so that you can build long-term relationships.

If you can't connect with your readers, you will lose them very quickly. This means your blog becomes a ghost town.

Creating Multiple Posts

Bullet points and list posts are some techniques that keep many blog readers around.

These techniques allow writers to work on several posts at one time. This is great for productivity.

Here are some ways you can write many posts at one time:

- When you start writing a post and get writer's block, begin writing another one. The point here is to not stop writing. Put every blog on a new page or document. By doing this, when you are ready to start writing again, you will know where you need to begin. Make a log with incomplete blog posts. There is no telling how many times I have begun a post, forgot that I did, and wound up writing it all over again.

- Choose a central location to keep a list of post ideas. Everybody knows that ideas can come from anywhere at any time. You need to know where you have stored all your ideas whether they are good, bad, or whatever. Keep a running list, when you happen to get writer's block, you'll have some ideas to get you started again.

- Write down random thoughts, phrases, and words you want to put into future posts. When you build a house, you have to build the foundation first. When writing a blog post, you don't have to begin with the foundation. Just a random thought is a great place to start.

- Don't do too much research. Some strong posts can be well researched and thought out. It might get to a point when enough is enough. Sometimes writing can't happen by itself. Your next blog might not exist if you take the time to research each tiny detail. You can be accurate but set a time limit on how long you are going to research the subject. Once you have hit your time limit, add some links and work on it another day.

Bloggers are usually good jugglers and can handle many projects at one time but there are times when you just need to sit back, relax, and let the words flow naturally.

Integrating Facebook

Whether you tolerate it, hate it, or love it, you just can't forget how successful Facebook has been. In some markets where it is dominating the web, it is catching up and just might succeed.

Sometimes we forget that there was just an internet before Facebook came along. Many people had websites or blogs before Facebook was ever thought about. Using Facebook is a good way to get some exposure for your blog's content. You might republish your blog onto Facebook or you could use Facebook Connect to add Facebook's profile and log in to your site.

Here are some ideas as for how to integrate your blog or website with Facebook:

XHTML or Custom CMS Site

Many people use either something coded in Django, Ruby, XHTML/PHP or a custom CMS. The Facebook Developer Wiki gives you a lot of information if you use any of these.

Facebook has also introduced Facebook Connect Playground and Facebook Connect Wizard that makes integrating Facebook onto your site much easier. It also gives you widgets and sample codes for Facebook buttons, comment boxes, and much more.

Wordpress

The most popular publishing platform around is WordPress. You would think that integrating Facebook into WordPress would be easy.

It can be. It has many different plugins but it takes some time and effort to get everything set up. Don't fear for there are some tools and resources to help integrate WordPress with Facebook.

- *"Sociable Facebook Connect"*
  Sociable.es has a plugin for Facebook Connect. It gets updated frequently and has a lot of features. You can add boxes to show recent visitors to your site along with friends and people who make comments. Be warned that this plugin will make new users for any Facebook Connect users that come to your blog.

- *"WPBook"*
  This has some unique features. First and foremost you can cross-post all your blog onto Facebook. Second, any comments that get posted on one site will show up on the other. This means if someone leaves a comment on Facebook, it will show up on your blog post, too. This is handy for people who want to show their content to many users but don't want to keep track of all the different conversations.

- *"WordPress/Facebook Connect"*
  This plugin was created by Adam Hupp, a Facebook engineer. It hasn't been updated

that much but it does give ways to integrate WordPress and Facebook Connect. By doing this, users can use Facebook to leave comments on your site. This will show you their profile picture so you know who it was at a glance.

- Add Your Blog Feed
  If you aren't worried about getting comments, and just want to show your blog on Facebook, Six Apart's easy guide lets you add your blog feed. It is intended for users of TypePad. It's a good read for anybody that uses a blog platform that has RSS support.

TypePad/Movable Type

There are two blogging platforms offered by Six Apart. One is Movable Type that you host yourself. The other is TypePad that is hosted by others. Six Apart released *"Facebook Connect Commenters"* plugin for Movable Type last year. This allows users to log in with their Facebook login. From there, they can leave comments and share these actions with Facebook.

TypePad has built Facebook compatibility into their newest release. It lets you post from your blog directly onto Facebook. You can show updates and let users comment using either their Twitter or Facebook identity.

Joomla and Drupal

These are the most popular open source content management systems. Both of these offer many features that are useful for bigger sites and large communities.

Drupal is used when a bigger community site is needed. Since most of these sites have existing users with profiles, adding Facebook is attractive for these users. Nobody wants to have to create another account just to leave a comment on a site they've visited. Site owners like it because it allows them to build a larger community.

There are several plugins for Drupal. Here are some of the better ones:

- *"Drupal for Facebook"*
  This lets users log in to your site with your Facebook login but it uses Drupal to push its site content to Facebook and to make applications for Facebook. This has been around for over two years.

- *"Drupal Facebook Connect"*
  This module works with Facebook Connect to add logins to an existing Drupal site. Users can just use their login for Facebook to see which Facebook friends have accounts on a particular Drupal site. It lets them publish content onto their Facebook page. Users can also ask Facebook friends to join a particular Drupal site. This is great for anybody who has apps backed by Drupal.

- *"Drupal Facebook Connect Module"*
  This is a great option for users who have Drupal that would like to add Facebook Connect logins to their already existing site.

With Joomla, *"jwFacebook Comments 1.5"* lets owners of sites add a comment box for Facebook to the bottom of Joomla entries.

Conclusion

Thanks for making it through to the end of *How to Start a Blog*. Let's hope it was informative and able to provide you with all of the tools you need to achieve your goals whatever they may be.

The next step is to pick out a niche that you would love to write about for the rest of your life. Use the information in this book to make sure that you create an entertaining blog that you will love and that others will love. You don't want to be another statistic.

Finally, if you found this book useful in any way, a review on Amazon is always appreciated!

How to Write a Blog

*The Best Technique
to Plan and Write
Amazing Blog Posts
for Growing Your
Community 10X*

Table of Contents

facts and as such any inattention, use or misuse of the information in question by the reader will render any resulting actions solely under their purview. There are no scenarios in which the publisher or the original author of this work can be in any fashion deemed liable for any hardship or damages that may befall them after undertaking information described herein.

Additionally, the information in the following pages is intended only for informational purposes and should thus be thought of as universal. As befitting its nature, it is presented without assurance regarding its prolonged validity or interim quality. Trademarks that are mentioned are done without written consent and can in no way be considered an endorsement from the trademark holder.

Mark Gray

Mark Gray is an online marketer expert in monetization with more than 10 years of experience in selling digital and physical high ticket products with blogs.

After his IT engineering degree, Mark started to work for one of the top 5 techs multinational company in the world. At the same time, he started to study the rules of marketing because he wanted to understand how a multinational company has become as it is.

He immediately understood the potentiality of applying the concepts of marketing but online.

After various years of mistakes, miss-understanding and loss of money, Mark finally quitted his highly paid job to focus himself in creating multiple sources of income.

Now he has several 6-figure online businesses and he finally decides to explain how he gained his results.

Introduction

The following chapters will discuss ways to make sure that you create high-quality articles for your blog. You can put money and effort into creating an amazing looking blog. You can even work hard at driving in traffic through ads and social media. However, if you can't deliver on content, people will not stay.

The first chapter will dive on how you can drive traffic to your blog and find the right readers and customers. If you don't get the right readers, your monetization efforts will probably not pay off.

In the next chapter, we will discuss picking the right niche for your blog and making the right arguments for your audience.

The longest chapter will talk about writing viral posts. This is what everybody wants to know how to do. It makes or breaks your blog. If you can't write an amazing article, then what's the point of wasting your time creating the blog?

The last few chapters will help you stay successful. We'll go through how to stay motivated, make scheduled posts, come up with a writing team, connect with other famous brands, and present giveaways to help your social presence.

Let's not waste any more time. Let's get started writing a famous and successful blog.

How to Have a Famous Blog

Most people out there that want to create a blog also seeks fame and success. Fame and success are closely related. If you are famous, chances are you are also successful. In this chapter, you will be learning how to be both.

Free and user-friendly blogging software has created a virtual soapbox for everybody. But for some individuals and small businesses, creating a successful blog means getting their word out to be heard by others. This means they are serving readers, not bombarding them with a bunch of marketing materials.

The best way to create a loyal following is to come up with useful content that your readers will consume and share with others.

Begin with a Personal Blog

If you are interested in becoming famous, the best starting point is a personal blog. Personal blogs are all about yourself. As such, all it needs is your name for the URL.

Figure the Purpose of Your Blog and Stick to it

You need to define what your readers want to learn, and then, come up with a strategy on how you can reach them. You need to be true on your blog goals. Are you going to provide readers with product information? Are you planning on provoking a conversation? Will you be commenting on trending topics? Any approach is valid, but you need to figure out the value you are going to give to your audience and continue delivering them. If you create a blog post that isn't useful or share-worthy, it isn't going to produce a lot of value for you or your readers.

Solve Your Readers Problems

You have probably read and heard this before, but it must be reiterated that this is the most effective way to become successful. Problem-solving websites and blogs tend to become successful the fastest compared to others. Most people don't enjoy reading blogs that are just about a person bragging about something. They want to find something helpful, valuable, and useful.

It's important that you are a problem solver in whatever field you choose. There are problems everywhere. All you need to do is think of a solution and share it. By helping other people reach success, you will also reach success.

Use Social Media

It's important to make the most out of social media. Always include a "share" button for Google+, Reddit, LinkedIn, Twitter, and Facebook on your blog. The easier it is for your readers to share content, the more likely they are to do so.

Make Friends with Other Bloggers

It is extremely helpful to create relationships with others in your field. It is also a great way to learn more. By communicating with more experienced people and learning from their mistakes, you will end up becoming even better at what you do. When you make blogger friends, more people are going to learn your name. Sooner or later everybody will know who you are.

SEO-Friendly Content

You must get smart about your search engine optimization. Figure the keywords for your subject matter that people often search, and then, figure the best way to use them in the title and body of your post.

The earlier these keywords appear, the higher your post will be on a Google search. As an example, "Hiring the Best Plumber: Eight Things to Look At" is going to get a better ranking than "Eight things to Look at When Hiring a Plumber." This is because plumber comes earlier in the first example. It's also a good idea to keep your blog titles under 120 characters so that people will be able to tweet them easily.

The most important variables when it comes to Google rankings are the authority and the number of the sites that link a post. A stronger website linking to you means better influence and ranking in Google. The more useful your content is, the better are your odds for other sites to link it.

Speak the Language of Your Audience

This is often a problem for marketers that start blogging. Their first few posts will always come out like a press release and not like a conversation. You will get the most benefit, both from an engagement and an SEO perspective, when you use terms that will resonate with your readers. It's important that you don't write a blog that will impress your college English professor. You need to impress your customer instead.

Promote Yourself and Your Blog

Promoting is one of the best and most direct ways to make your blog more popular. A lot of people tend to skip this step and believe that it's not that important. Promotion shines up a business. Promotion is what places a movie at the top of the box office. Promotion is what makes things popular. You should not skip on promotion.

Promotion nowadays has become even more important for blogs. There are many different blogs out there that are going to fall into your niche, making it hard to stand out. There is only one way to overcome this problem and that is to write amazing content and promote the crap out of yourself and your blog.

Be a Part of the Conversation on Your Blog as Well as Others

This goes hand and hand with creating friendships with other bloggers. You should try to drive traffic to other blogs, and you should try to respond to both good and bad comments about your blog. If you let people comment on your blog, make sure you can handle the negative feedback. If you don't allow comments on your blog, learn to expect that they will appear somewhere else.

People are going to talk about you, your company, and your products whether you want them or not. Blogging is just another social business strategy and it provides a great way to engage with consumers. This creates an amazing opportunity to exchange ideas and information with existing and prospective customers.

Serve Your Readers like a Waiter

This may seem a bit odd, but it's true. Everybody has seen waiters and waitresses treat their customers very well. As a blogger, you should serve your readers that way because readers are the only thing that will make your blog popular and successful. You cannot forget about your readers.

In the end, becoming famous isn't what is important. What is important is how valuable, helpful, and friendly you are. Like I said earlier, people don't visit your blog to read everything amazing in your life. They are there to read some cool stuff that will help them become successful.

It's important to always seek excellence because that will lead you to success. Also, and this is very, very important, success will not come overnight. It is going to take a long time and a lot of work to become successful and famous.

Picking the Best Niche

It seems like almost everybody has a blog nowadays. With around 42 million WordPress blogs online, it will not be that difficult to find information on the craziest of topics. It is now your turn to create a successful blog. I hope you're excited.

But how does this crazy system work? How are you going to generate traffic, build your following, and monetize the blog? There is one important thing that you forgot. Amid the excitement, you knock everything else to the side from branding, color choice, plugins, and theme layout, to pumping out blog posts.

Before you know it, you have created a 2,000-word post on how great homeschooling is. You followed it up with a 1,800-word article on how to gain social media tractions. You're all set. You published your first one, sent it out to the social-sphere, and jumped right back into writing more posts.

While you understand that it will take some time to get noticed, you also see that the blog is not getting any traffic or engagement. You've got amazing content and you've shared it on social media. What went wrong? It doesn't matter how good your blog looks or how easily people can navigate it. If you don't figure out this one thing, you are going to have a very hard time finding engagement and traction.

You need a niche.

Simply put, a niche is a topic that you write about. It is the main theme of the blog. When you figure out a niche, every single post will revolve around it and that's pretty much all you talk about.

But why would somebody want to do that? Are readers not going to get bored reading about the same thing all the time? Wouldn't you become bored having to write about the same topic each week?

No.

Most people will find blogs that they enjoy because it gives them specific content that they like. For example, if you visit the blog *Pen to Paper*, you would find that their posts are all about writing tips and tricks, as well as book reviews. Since they stick to topics on writing, they have created a spot in the writing world.

There are a lot of different blogs out there, but most of them can be broken down into two categories: niche blogs and multi-topic or general blogs.

Niche blogs mainly focus on one topic, while general blogs focus on several different topics. A lifestyle blog is an example of a multi-topic one.

When it comes to a blog like this, you will often find a wide array of content on basic lifestyle topics like fitness, health, décor, technology, and career. *PopSugar* is a good example of this type of blog.

You might think that creating a general blog is the better choice because it covers a lot of topics, making it easier to attract different people. It's not. *ShoutMeLoud* said multi-topic blogs are bad for monetization, readership, and SEO. Although bad may not be the right word and *PopSugar* is obviously not hurting, properly running a multi-topic blog is a pretty big deal for smaller bloggers.

But when you have a niche blog, you get a lot of other benefits.

1. Niches keep you on track.

Blogging is going to be harder than you think. You will have to pump valuable and awesome content on a regular basis if you plan to see any amount of traffic coming your way. Often, people will lose focus. Bloggers' block will happen, and your creative juices will dry up.

You might not know this, but you are going to have more tools available when you have a niche. You will be able to look at the popularity of your posts and repurpose them from a fresh angle. When you have a niche blog, you will also be able to come up with topics and headlines a lot easier.

2. You become an expert.

Since you understand your niche, writing about it should be simple. Most things that you write about will likely be original or is going to be based on your own experiences. You can also pick something that you're interested in and become an expert through blogging. Soon, others will visit your blog to learn important tips and tricks.

3. Your audience will grow.

People want quality content and they are going to seek blogs that meet their needs. When you have a niche blog, it will fit nicely with people because you are able to give them relatable and consistent content. They will come to know what your niche is and learn from what you have done. In the end, they will want your personal view of things.

You will also end up having a better chance of holding onto your readers if you create content in your niche. For example, if you write a viral health post, people are going to expect another health-related content the next time they return. If you end up writing about the best-kept beauty secrets next, there will be a good chance that people will not stick around. That makes it harder to build a reliable audience when you have a general blog.

4. Monetization becomes easier.

Whether you started your blog with the idea of making money or not, you will soon realize that you can try making some income with the right audience. Some common ways of monetizing are through affiliate programs and AdSense, but a better way to maximize success is to build an email subscriber list using a lead magnet. Once you attract a target audience with a lead magnet, you will be able to build an email list even faster, creating a chance for repeat visits and monetization.

Picking Your Niche

Now that you know that it's important to have a niche, how do you go about picking the right one? Your niche needs to occur through your passion, revenue potential, and knowledge. When all three align, that's your niche.

1. What is your passion?

For most bloggers, their blogs are their guilty pleasure. It's the thing they do when they have free time. For your blog to flourish, you must have passion when you come up with your posts every week. Your blog could live for years or decades, so ask yourself if you are going to be able to write about your niche for 10 straight years?

Are you going to still have the same passion several years down the road? Blogging can take a toll on people. If you can't stick with your niche and keep that level of excitement with your first post, you probably will not have all that much luck growing it.

2. Do I have knowledge about my topic?

How long your blog lasts will all depend on your knowledge in that niche. Powerhouse blogs such as Derek Halpern's *Social Triggers* or Neil Patel's *QuickSprout* have hundreds of pages of content about something they understand from inside out.

You may have it in your head that you must know everything about your topic before you start, but that's not necessarily true. The blog *Smart Passive Income* was created by Pat Flynn, and he didn't know anything about it when he started.

His blog started as a way to keep notes while studying for the LEED program. He was quickly able to become an expert with AdSense, which moved him into generating passive income, which was yet another niche that he mastered.

So, if you are passionate about something or are interested in something you just found, you will be able to learn as you go and earn your authority.

3. Will it have revenue potential?

Not everything niche will be profitable. There are some that are too narrow to have a big audience, or too broad to have a loyal one. You might also find it hard to come up with new content.

Here are some factors that you need to take into consideration.

- What is the competition?

- Are other bloggers making any money?

- Are there any CPA offers or affiliate programs?

- How easy is it to attract advertisers?

- What are your resources?

If your plan is to have a profitable blog, you need to start thinking about profitable niches. With the right amount of resources, time, and luck, any niche can make you money. But why make your life difficult when you could just pick a profitable niche.

As a rule of thumb, if there are a lot of high-tick services and goods for sale in a niche or if it has high customer value, you have probably discovered a good one. Everybody knows that lawyer's fees, health care, and bills are expensive, so it's not a surprise that a niche in the medical, dental, and legal fields is going to be profitable.

Insurance is another profitable niche. Automotive insurance can be fairly cheap month-to-month. For an insurance company though, a customer that stays with them for several years and buys more insurance is going to be worth tens of thousands.

There are several different ways to validate the profitability of a niche. If you are in doubt, the easy way to validate is to research the niche market's keywords and industry trends.

When you're in a niche where the majority of the keywords have a large cost per click, it tells you that advertisers are willing to spend a lot of money to make a sale. This typically means that your niche is going to be profitable.

Myth About Niches

1. You find a niche and then niche it down.

No, not really. It's a decent advice because narrowing down will help you find a very specific audience that is able to relate to your writing. But does that make it necessary? No.

The Best Blog Niches

To help you get an idea of some good niches, here are a few examples.

1. How to make money

This is an obvious one. Most beginners will often find themselves asking if they should write a blog about making money. It's a good question because these are the blogs that tend to make a lot of money. Luckily, this is not the one and only niche that will make money, but it is the easiest.

It is the easiest if you can prove that you are making the money yourself. A lot of bloggers jump into this niche and go at it the wrong way. They pretend to have the information on how to make money online, but their readers are not stupid. They know there are other options. So, if you are not able to prove to them that you practice what you preach, you are not going to make any money.

But that doesn't beginners can't be successful in this niche. It should be approached as a blog journey. Chronicle the things that work for you and what doesn't. Let others follow along on your journey.

2. Health and Fitness

This is a tricky niche because you can get a great deal of traffic from it, but can also be quite hard to monetize if you don't know how to do it right. To start off, affiliate marketing would be a great monetization effort. This works well because your audience is looking for solutions to problems and Amazon probably has something for them.

3. Food

Making money through this is quite hard because the audience is not typically looking to purchase anything. They want recipes. The best way to approach this is to use ads to help supplement.

4. Beauty and Fashion

This is probably the holy grail of successful blogs because you can make a lot of money and end up gaining access to amazing events. The problem is that it can be extremely hard. While other blogs rely on written content, beauty and fashion rely more on your personality and your ability to put yourself out there. A lot of bloggers in this niche will focus on Instagram and YouTube since they are more visual platforms.

People will create blogs for various reasons, but eventually, they are going to want to monetize them. When you have a niche, you can create a plan, build credibility, and increase your audience to make it easier to earn income. With a lot of passion and knowledge about a topic and its potential for income, finding a niche should be easy.

Writing Viral Posts

Imagine being super excited about writing content for your blog. You spend days working on a post. Once it's published, you see these results:

- 0 comments

- 0 shares

- 2 page views

Guess what? Those two page views are from you checking any typos. That hurts. If it keeps happening, it's going to get really frustrating. I'm sure you're an amazing writer, but if you don't approach your blog the right way, it's not going to spread.

You need to approach it from a marketing perspective. If you are not strategic with your posts, they are not going to get any results and they definitely won't help build your business. You don't have to give up though. This chapter will look at several ways to write viral blog posts.

It can be hard to create a blog post that ends up going viral. There isn't a secret sauce to making it happen, but there are a lot of things that can make your odds higher.

Having a popular blog is a huge asset. It will feel amazing to make and it will bring attention to the things that you are doing. The problem happens when nobody reads your post. It's not useful to anybody but you. You can do a quick search online and find tons of suggestions on how to drive traffic to your blog. The problem is very few are as good as they say they are. The only true way to drive traffic and create a popular blog is by creating amazing content that will change the lives of your readers. It means you have to put yourself out there and create a connection. Content is king, but without the right spark, even the best will lie dormant.

What is a Viral Post?

This is the holy grail of blog writing because everybody is buzzing about it and is sharing it to everyone they know. The problem is that so many people define viral by a crazy high number in the millions because of highly publicized prank videos and music. But when defined as such, it makes going viral unrealistic and nearly impossible for blog content. You probably already understand that you will never reach those numbers. You need to define what going viral means to you.

A viral blog is typically defined by how many times it is shared by people. With social media, there is greater potential for any type of content to become viral. Videos and photos are more likely to go viral, and you can easily incorporate these into your post. These are the types of photos that you see all over Facebook, and the videos that get millions of hits on YouTube. Moreover, viral content will help you get a lot of high-quality backlinks and more exposure to a bigger audience.

Since you need to define your own viral meaning, what would your numbers be? To come up with a reasonable number, you have to figure out your average post shares. For example, if your average post is normally shared around 10 to 20 times on Facebook, then you would go viral at 200 Facebook shares and higher. For a different blogger, the number could be more than 500.

What Makes Things go Viral?

In order for a post to go viral, it needs to strike a chord that lots of your readers are able to resonate with. Most of the time, viral content will have one or more of these qualities:

- Useful and unique

- Trendy or popular topic

- Controversial

- Funny

Not very many blogs have each of these features. You should just aim for one or two. Having cute and funny pictures of children and pets are always popular. Controversial topics are also popular. But your blog may not deal with these types of things. Rumors tend to spread quickly like in high school.

This should not be your goal. You want a legitimate and helpful blog, not one that spreads false rumors just for popularity. I'm just using this as an example of things that tend to spread quickly. You can become viral without lying.

At this point, you may be thinking that writing a post that goes viral is complete luck.

Well, until it is not. Chances are, once you get the hang of this, you will know when one of your posts is going to go viral. You know what you've done, and you will be able to repeat them. It might not happen with every post, but with the majority of them.

Typically, when a blogger strives in vain for success, they have skipped or are not aware of the three blogging fundamentals. Let's get those out of the way.

   1.   Knowing your niche.

We covered the importance of having a niche in the last chapter, but there so many bloggers that forget about this. That's why earlier in this chapter I added: "but your blog may not deal with these types of things." No matter how easy certain types of content can go viral, if it doesn't fit into your niche, don't write about it.

You want to come off as an expert in your niche. This will not happen if you are constantly throwing random topics into your articles. Let's say you write a diet blog, specifically on the ketogenic diet. A timely issue, however, pushes you to write a political post that you know will go viral. Your readers are still going to read on the keto diet and now they are reading something about politics in your blog. They are likely to be annoyed because now they can't find a recipe for supper. They are going to view you as a less reliable source for information on the keto diet.

Now, you can pay attention to news and information concerning your niche and post blogs about that. It's important that you do because your readers are going to turn to you to refute or agree with what the news is saying. Let's say you write about billiards, you will want to share upcoming events and news. A great way to stay up-to-date on these things is to set up a Google news alert with different keywords that work with your niche. If the niche is billiards, keywords like pool and billiards will work. If the niche is the keto diet, keywords like ketogenic and keto will work. Google will then send you the relevant articles.

When you know your niche, and stick to it, you will be able to come up with content that your readers actually want to read. They will then start to see you as an expert and a person they can trust.

2. Knowing the community.

Let's assume that you understand your niche like the back of your hand, but the content still isn't spreading. The next thing people often forget about is understanding the community within their niche. You need to figure out where your readers hang out online. Start visiting popular blogs within your niche. Read through the things they talk about in the comments, especially for popular topics. Start getting involved and provide them with helpful input in the comment section without mentioning anything about your blog.

The more involved you become, the more likely it is that other commenters are going to click your name and find your blog. As you start learning about your community, you will be able to tailor your content for them. You will be able to figure out what makes them laugh, cry, happy or angry. Above everything else, you will discover what will make them want to share your content.

If you are able to figure out why your community likes to share certain information, you will be able to frame your posts to pique their interest. You will also find out that readers share content that they can relate to, motivates them, and makes them feel better. Start digging deeper and you will find that readers are going to share things that they are dealing with. They are discovering new ways to succeed and be happy despite such obstacles.

When you are able to find the content that is spreading, try to find common denominators. Are these posts about certain lifestyles or situations funny or serious? Come up with a list of what readers share the most because that is what they like to read.

This doesn't mean you have to sell out! It means that you have learned what your community wants. They share your posts because you understand them. The best compliment you can give your readers is to let them know that you appreciate and understand them. This can be done by writing posts that they want. But you can only do this if you are active in your community.

3. Knowing the worldview

The last thing people skip over is understanding their worldview. This is one of the most important parts of blog writing. The worldview is the way we view things, and what we think about those things. It's your own opinion. The way you view the world sets you apart from everyone else. It is going to attract readers to keep reading your articles, or it could end up causing them to reject your blog.

You probably already know your worldview. But have you figured out how to express this view in such a way that your readers will be able to appreciate and relate to? Unfortunately, there are people who have not realized how their worldview will affect those around them. If a writer often rubs people the wrong way, it is likely because of the way they present their worldview.

For example, you may think that the sky is green but everybody else thinks it's blue. You share your belief in a way that discredits everybody else's belief. This will often happen by accident because the writer doesn't realize how their view affects other people.

You need to know the difference between your view and other people's view. If you say something like "The sky is green, not blue, and anybody that thinks it's blue is stupid," you're going to lose a lot of readers. You can modify this point to be more thought-provoking instead of rude, such as "The sky may appear blue, but what if it were actually green?" In this way, people won't feel discredited, and they will likely feel more compelled to consider your point of view.

When you share your views this way, you will seem more considerate and understanding. This is what is going to make you more likable and your post to likely go viral. The more people that can see your beliefs in your content, the more likely they will be to share your posts.

Inclusivity, Community, and Niche

The first tip to writing a viral post is to make sure that the three above-mentioned things are combined. If you really look at a successful blog, you will find that the writer knows their niche and community, and they share an inclusive worldview. They make their opinions matter to their readers.

Spreading the Word

The following are ways to get your blog under the noses of more readers:

- Add it to your newsletter.

- Add links to past and future blog posts.

- Use social bookmarking.

- Add to relevant forum comments.

- Provide SEO for images.

- Post your article to LinkedIn.

- If applicable, post it to Pinterest.

- If applicable, post it to YouTube.

- Post it on Google+.

- Post it on Facebook.

- Post it on Twitter.

- Post your article in forums on your niche.

- Submit it to Mix, which took over StumbleUpon.

- Submit the post to Reddit.

There's no need to do all every time, but the more places that you share your post on, the more eyes will see it. You will quickly be able to figure out what is working for you.

Writing Formula

The following is a simple formula to make sure that your posts are search engine optimized.

1. The Headline

The main purpose of your posts is to have visitors read the whole thing and then act. Your whole article is important, but if you don't have an attention-grabbing headline to bring readers in, it's not going to matter. This is the reason why a lot of marketers say that 80% of your advertising should be spent on the headline. If you use the right process, it won't be that hard to do.

Start by writing down your top-level idea. A lot of people will tell you that you need to create your headline once you have written your article, but that's not the best advice. When you make the headline first, it will provide you with a direction for the rest of your article. You need to write at least three top-level ideas that you want people to learn from your article. From there, you can create your attention-grabbing headline. The following are eight principles for creating the best headlines:

- Ask your readers a question that relates directly to your product and make them answer it.

- o *"If you earned $1,000 or more on the side doing things you already know, what would you do?"*

- When you can't think of anything else, use a "how" headline.

  - o *"How to discover your dream job?"*

- Tell an inspiring story.

  - o *"A mistake that costs a small business $3,000 a year."*

- Use lists as a headline.

  - o *"8 mistakes that even job counselors make."*

- Announce something that is relevant and novel to your reader.

  - o *"Finally, a way to make extra money that isn't sleazy."*

- Create an urgent or time-sensitive headline.

  - o *"Discover 7 reasons why most businesses fail before I get rid of this free report forever."*

- Give your audience useful information.

- o *This free guide will show you 7 mistakes that keep people from getting their dream job."*

- Stir up some mystery.

  - o *"Do Washington insiders know about this hidden tax that is siphoning off 13% of your earnings?"*

By this point, you should have a good idea of what your headline is going to be. You can pump it up more a little later.

2. Create an Outline

A big problem beginner bloggers have is getting words on paper. The problem is that they don't normally have any direction on what they want to write and they spend hours trying to figure out their structure and flow. You can fix this problem with a simple outline.

You may be thinking how a simple outline is going to help you come up with an article, but you'll be amazed at how faster you can write when you have a guideline on want to cover.

To help you out, here is a template for an outline:

Headline

Introduction

- *Come up with a hook that will grab the readers' attention.*

Part 1

- *Point 1*
- *Point 2*
- *Point 3*

Part 2

- *Point 1*
- *Point 2*
- *Point 3*

Part 3

- *Point 1*
- *Point 2*
- *Point 3*

Conclusion

Once you have created your outline, you should have around 80% of your article written.

3. Tying Everything Together

By now you have already done most of the work, and you now need to place it into a blog format.

This doesn't mean typing it up on your platform. Instead, it means writing it in a way that your readers will understand and enjoy. There are two things that you need to do in order to achieve this:

- Don't write about things that you have not experienced. There is plenty of spun content and unhelpful advice on the internet, so there's no need to muddy the waters further Everybody has experiences that they are able to share.

- Write as if you are talking to your friends. Nobody is going to enjoy reading academic jargon that is just going to put them to sleep. This is the reason why most marketing gurus will talk about the power of storytelling.

That's it. You have now come up with a blog post that has the chance to become viral. Just to make sure that you have everything under control, here are a few things to consider.

- Try not to fret over the length. Just try to make sure you have included everything you need to tell. As a rule of thumb, something under 800 words is going to be worthless, but you also shouldn't write something that is 10,000 words long.

- Images will help. Screenshots that show results can help, especially if it deals with a technical topic. Also, people love funny photos.

- Bolding important things will also help. This isn't necessary, but it does help grab people's attention.

- Make sure that you have a call to action at the end of your blog. These are things like check out my site, email me, sign-up for my course and follow me.

SPACE Post

This is the last way to create a viral post. Blogger Jordan Roper came up with this idea to help make her blog posts go viral, and all you have to remember is the word SPACE.

1. Specific

You have to understand your ideal reader and tailor your writing to them. This is something I've said before, and it is one of the most important things to do. Being specific means you know your niche and you know who your readers are.

2. Personality

Boring articles could get a few clicks, but it's not going to create fans. If you showcase your personality and create a brand for yourself, you will gain fans and loyal followers. Personality makes your content feel real to your readers and they will be able to connect with it more. You shouldn't make your articles dull just because you are afraid of being disliked or judged. The truth is not everybody will like you, and that's okay. So be you, and put your real personality into your writing. Also, don't forget what I mentioned earlier. While you should put your personality into your writing, you should also try your best to be inclusive. You don't want to make your readers feel like they don't matter even if they don't see things as you do.

3. Actionable

Fluff isn't going to build you a following. You need to give your readers actionable steps that they can do to accomplish what you are teaching them. Step-by-step tutorials are a great way to do this. Providing them with screenshots of your work will also help. People like seeing things, so you can't go wrong when you add in videos and images. In-depth content will be more effective than surface-level content.

4. Comprehensive

Choose something that you are able to cover in its entirety. You are looking to answer your reader's questions, not create more. This will often mean that you will have to write a long-form blog post. A blog between 1500 to 2500 words is a good goal, but that doesn't mean you have stick to a certain number of words.

5. Evergreen

This means you create content that will remain relevant years from now. This means you should not use the advice that is going to be different in a week. Your readers should be able to keep coming back and still find your work helpful. This doesn't mean every single blog is going to be evergreen.

In the end, setting a goal for your blog to go viral is great, but you also need to understand that not everything you create will go viral. It can be hard to predict when things are going to go viral, so keep an open mind and work hard. The only thing you can do is try to increase your chances by using some or all of the tips in this chapter.

Staying Motivated

Remaining motivated to continue blogging is not easy. Sitting down to a blank page each day and writing to an invisible audience that might not engage can be challenging. To keep you motivated blogging for the long run, here are some tactics to help your willpower:

- You must respond to comments. It is hard to get people to share or comment on your posts. It is important to show that you are taking part in the conversation. You need to respond to every comment with more than just saying "Thanks." You have to encourage others to engage with you and share your information.

- Encourage employees, friends, and family to share your posts. Every person you know has social media contacts. It might only be 25 more people, but it is 25 more than you had before. NEVER BEG. Instead, give current readers reasons to continue to share your content. Show them respect.

- Find a blogging buddy. Find a friend who also blogs and gets support from them. You can help each other by cheering each other on. You can look over and edit each other's posts.

- Go to your page every day at the same time. For many writers, this will either be first thing each morning or right before you go to bed.

- Start writing in public. For a change of pace, take your computer or tablet and go to a local park or coffee shop. Your creative juices will begin to flow.

- Stop writing words. Begin using videos or images to make your blogs. This will change things up for you and your audience.

- Use your smartphone to record thoughts and ideas when you are on the go. Don't think you will remember them all. You won't.

- Answer your readers' questions. This works great for all types of businesses. Create a list of questions your audience or customers have had.

- Get ideas from employees. You can install a suggestions box in the employee break room. Gather these little tidbits of information and utilize what you have found.

- If you don't know what your audience wants to read, just ask them.

- Talk with other authors in your same field of expertise. This will help you get attention by associating with them. They might even help you promote your content.

- Tap into current controversies. Give your perspective or opinion on a hot topic.

- Go to live events. You can use these to engage with other bloggers and gather new ideas for your blog.

- Utilize social media to your benefit. Answer questions about groups and ask questions on Facebook to gather information. This might give you new ideas or material for new posts.

- Participate in Twitter chats. You can either start a post to prepare for a chat or respond to one that is already going.

- Comment on other blogs. This might start a conversation that can continue on your blog as well.

- Look at your analytics. Find what topics and posts resonate well with your readers. This might help you brainstorm new ideas.

- Break down your post to two or more. Don't try to pack everything into one post. It is important to provide value, but never try to put everything upfront. This is easy to see when you have written an epic post. This doesn't mean that just because you have written it, you have to publish it.

Staying motivated while blogging requires many different tactics to help you build a habit. As your blog and readers grow, your ability to increase your willpower will grow too.

Scheduling Posts

If you want to show your blog has authority, you need to publish content regularly. If you would like to know how you can schedule blog posts regularly, keep reading for the best ways possible.

Before you check plans of publishing the next blog post, you need to know how important it is to do. This will show you are interested in scheduling the task.

Why is Scheduling Needed?

Blogging is a journey where you have to update regularly. Consistency does matter to make you stand out in the crowd. It pleases the search engines too.

Scheduling the next post is necessary because you don't want any followers to miss it just because you didn't get it published on time. By using WordPress, scheduling your posts is a lot easier.

Other than scheduling your posts, you need to set up a frequency to show your subscribers when you will be submitting new content. Social media will highlight your new posts if you share them on these forums.

Genuine followers and loyal subscribers who look forward to reading your next post will wait for it as you have it scheduled. You might wonder why you should schedule posts when you can publish one from anywhere now. This is why blogging is so powerful. You are not tied to just one place or one desk. You can blog from anywhere you would like.

There might be times when you don't have the time to blog because you are traveling or attending to family matters. If you are sick or need to help care for somebody in your family, you are not going to have the time to think about publishing your blog.

During the times you can't post new articles, your blog will simply be bare. If you move your posts to a scheduling calendar, your blog will remain active even if you are not. WordPress can make scheduling your upcoming posts very easy with this built-in feature.

Default Schedule Method

If you run your blog on WordPress, you don't have to worry about scheduling your posts. They offer an easy and simple solution that lets you add new posts without publishing them immediately. You can plan to post it at a later date or time. Before you do this, you have to set your time zone since WordPress uses UTC.

You can change this by going to Settings then find General on the Admin dashboard. You should see the field where you can find your time zone. You are now ready to schedule your posts. Just do the following steps.

When you have edited and updated your final draft, just find the section with the Publish button. Don't click the Publish button, instead find the Edit link that is beside "Publish immediately." Click this link. You can now set the date you want your post published. When you have chosen the date, click "Ok."

You will see the "Publish" button has changed to "Schedule." Click the "Schedule" button. Your post will now be published on the date you scheduled automatically. That was fairly easy, wasn't it?

You can use this scheduling option that WordPress offers and begin making a schedule for future posts. This method is great for a one author blog or a blog that only has a couple of posts published weekly.

If you run a blog that has many contributors with many different posts each day, WordPress has your back.

The Four Best Plugins That Will Publish Your Posts

The above scheduling option is great but you have to manually do that for every post. It is a huge task if you have many contributors or if you need to create a full calendar. When you have many contributors, there could be a chance for two or more posts to be scheduled on the same day and possibly at the same time. This won't help your blog. You need a system that schedules posts based on how frequent you need them published instead of times or dates. Let's look at some plugins that will give you these options.

- Editorial Calendar. Your blogging will become easier when you create a calendar schedule. All you need to do is draft all your new posts and go to "Calendar." Check the unscheduled posts and then drag and drop them on the calendar where you want them to be published. There is also a default option where WordPress schedules your posts. You can go back and edit or change the times or dates on the editorial calendar. If there are many contributors, you will be able to see all their blogs on the calendar and then schedule them as you see fit. They won't get mixed up with others.

- WP Scheduled Posts. This is the best extension when scheduling posts for a site that has many authors and administrators. This plugin was developed by a blog called "The Tech Journal." It is now available for any WordPress user absolutely free. You can make a scheduling calendar for posts and choose who has access to the plugin. This plugin gives you complete control of post type, category type, and user access. You can also do more things than just schedule posts. All the planned topics for publishing get displayed on the Admin bar and Dashboard. You have the choice of setting custom styles and templates in the Admin bar for any scheduled post.

- Auto Post Scheduler. If you want a plugin that will publish posts at normal intervals, then you need to check Auto Post Scheduler by *Super Blog Me*. This plugin lets you schedule your new posts. It also lets you recycle old ones. This works well with blogs that have many contributors and a lot of articles to be published daily. You just need to set the right interval and the scheduler will publish the posts automatically each day at the correct time. This WordPress plugin was designed to work with the auto blogging plugin. You can use them both to automate your blog.

- Schedule Posts Calendar. This is a fancy layout that you will find on the "Edit Post" page. It does come in handy because it shows you a pop-up calendar instead of the drop-down field. When the calendar pops up, you can choose the date and time you need to schedule your posts. You can hide the default time display. That's all there is to this plugin. It is better than the default option available on the WordPress blog.

Scheduling upcoming blog posts is a simple but necessary way to maintain your consistency. When you have a content strategy, you won't be disappointing your readers when you take a vacation. This gets you into a publishing routine that is needed to create a profitable blog.

The plugins mentioned above can help you create a calendar for WordPress. Choose them wisely and never install any plugin that is not needed or you will not use.

Creating a Writing Team

Are you finding it hard to publish your blog regularly? Do you think about bringing other bloggers? If you have a team of bloggers, the workload can be shared. This will keep your blog full of fresh and updated content.

Why Do You Need a Team?

Posting to your blog regularly isn't just a way to incorporate your content. It is also the main way to bring awareness and traffic to your business. If you are having a hard time updating your blog constantly, think about finding some help.

Making a good team of bloggers can make regular contributions smoother. When you share responsibility, you will be providing new content regularly to make sure that not one person will bear the burden of how successful the blog is.

Creating a successful team isn't just about selecting some people and assigning them things to write about. It doesn't matter how many people you have on your team. You have to keep them inspired to create content that is engaging. This is going to take attention and time.

Here are some tips on how to set up a team that will be engaged and passionate to follow through:

Assembling the Team

The main element when creating a team is to find people who want to write and have a burning passion for the industry. You are asking them for a commitment, and your team members need to be excited about participating.

Ask any potential members to fill out an application to see if they are going to be a good fit for the team. You might decide to launch the team with an in-person meeting by sending out formal invitations. Nothing makes a sense of purpose and enthusiasm like bonding time with the team.

You will be able to do a lot of things at this meeting. The main purpose is to let everyone know their roles and responsibilities. This way they will feel confident about being able to contribute regularly.

It is also a good way to create team camaraderie. This is essential when you want work that goes beyond required.

Each team member needs to agree on what their role is. Document it, sign it, and make copies. When they sign that official document, it reinforces how important this commitment is.

Facilitate Communication and Manage Workflow

Your team is a team because every member is equally important. Having this mentality will create a sense of responsibility and accountability among members. It lets people volunteer for certain posts, take up any slack if necessary and make sure there are reasons to write new posts and to attend meetings.

You can use tools such as the Edit Flow WordPress plugin to manage your workflow. It gives you a monthly calendar, allows the team to collaborate on posts, and sends notifications so everybody's assignments get done on time.

Other apps such as Facebook groups and Slack let teams share documents and communicate without having to be in the same room.

Create Resource Materials

It doesn't matter if you work on a post as a team or if you assign it to someone at a meeting. How-to guides and materials are the best way to keep your team on track.

When you have these resources, team members know how things work. It creates a sense of ownership and responsibility. It's a good way to make blogging easier for everyone.

These resources might include:

- Best practice guide to make sure blog posts have the same tone and format

- Etiquette guides

- Contact sheet

- Editorial calendar that gets refreshed regularly with input from others

- Blog posting process document

- Team responsibilities, mission, and blog content ratios

Keep these documents organized in a central location. You could store them in a Google Drive account that was made just for your team and is accessible anywhere. Think about assigning different permissions like read-only and edit to certain people based on their roles and abilities.

You have the ability to make notes on documents and collaborate at the same time. This makes it easier to write articles with multiple authors.

Assign an Editor

Every blog should have another set of eyes to look it over before it is published. It doesn't have to be one person. To make sure your blog is updated and posts are published when needed or moved around if necessary, it is important to assign an editor for the team.

The editor doesn't just read the posts to make sure they are grammatically correct. They also check on other writers to see if they are going to meet their deadlines. They also manage the editorial calendar.

Anyone on the team can either approve or veto an idea. The editor will ensure the right questions get asked and will make executive decisions when deciding to either hold a post or publish it early.

The editor also has the job of keeping the team inspired. An editor shares information to make sure everybody is also comfortable doing so by email or by brainstorming without notice. The editor needs to be somebody who is outgoing and who loves to talk since these types of chats could lead to some awesome content.

Have Meetings to Talk About Content

Meetings are normally the first thing that gets stopped when everyone gets busy. They are as important as delivering the goods to clients. Having regular meetings whether they be in video or in person is a necessity. Meetings will help build better relationships with all the workers. If they are done right with actions items and an agenda, meetings allow everyone to know what their responsibilities are for the coming week.

Meetings can help inspire creativity. You might have everybody present some ideas to talk about or play a quick little game. Try to keep the meetings fun. It will keep the team engaged.

You can also use a plugin like Idea Stream to help with brainstorming. You can also set up a group on Facebook where people can discuss and share topics so when you do have a meeting, everyone will be focused and energetic.

Report Blog Performance

You need to let the team know about the blog's performance. It makes sure that every week or month you are posting content that is relevant. It will give everybody responsibility and something they can look forward to.

Try to set goals that the team can rally around. This can inspire a little bit of competition like which post had the most views, which has been on the site the longest, or who had the most shares on social media.

You can use Google Analytics to help track performance and this ties in nicely if you use Google Drive accounts for your team. Everything is accessible with just one login and password. Google Analytics also works well with WordPress. It has a dashboard that shows how many visits the site had and which posts are doing the best.

Contact Established Brands

You might be wondering how you can start collaborating with others. Collaborations are a great way to work with other bloggers. They can introduce you to a whole new audience and increase traffic to your blog.

What is collaborating? This is not about doing giveaways or taking pictures of each other. A simple definition of a blogger to blogger collaborations is to put your brains together and create new content.

But how exactly do you initiate blogger to blogger collaborations? Let's find out.

The Blogger Needs to Be a Good Fit

The new blogger you would like to collaborate with doesn't have to be exactly like you. Your blog might be about exercises while the other blog might be about active wear. The demographics, however, need to be similar for both. You might be a visual blogger who likes to add photos to your posts. It would be great to collaborate with somebody who is a professional photographer. If your audience is mainly women who are between the age of 35 and 45, you wouldn't want to collaborate with a blogger whose audience is men between the ages of 20 and 30. It isn't going to benefit either one of you.

Brainstorm Ideas

If you start asking people to collaborate with you but can't give them any ideas, it isn't going to get anywhere. Every detail doesn't have to be nailed down at first. Just pitch a few ideas. If you want to blog about books, find a local author and propose a four-week series. Work on getting sponsors to give you gifts for photos. Work on finding a theme for the complete series too. You need to provide them with as many details as possible. The more details, the more the chances of getting other bloggers on board.

Outside the Box

Remember that collaborations are not giveaways. They are good ways to get new followers. These tools are great to use over and over again. You don't even have to be that creative. You just need to try harder.

Pitch Like Crazy

It is easy to pitch to bloggers you know but you might want to pitch to somebody you've never met. This is totally fine, but you need to be very professional and formal when you pitch to somebody new. You need to properly introduce yourself and make your ideas extremely clear.

Here is a sample you can look at if you need one:

"Hello (insert person's name)!

My name is (insert your name here). I am a (tell about your blog) blogger at (name of the website). I am a fan of what you are creating and would love to team up for a post when you have the time.

Here are some of my ideas (insert ideas here). The dates I am available are (insert dates here). I am pretty sure we could get (insert company name) to sponsor items for this collaboration.

Let me know what you are thinking. I look forward to working with you."

Change Your Idea If You Need To

Your idea might need to be revised if you are collaborating with a blogger that does not like it. You need to be flexible. You want the other blogger to bring their own ideas to the table to make it a hit.

A great site to check out is *Flock and Gabble*. They have wonderful collaboration guides that can help you figure things out. They also have a Collab Camp to help you out.

Here are five things you should ask any brand before collaborating with them:

What Do They Want You to Do?

Most of the time, the brand will state what type of work they want for their campaign in the first email they send you. On very rare occasions, they won't. The scope of work just means what you can deliver to the brand for a certain project. You might just collaborate with a particular brand for one post only. Sometimes they might want a complete post that is seen on all social networks. Ask them how many posts they want and on which platforms.

The brand might also ask for analytics after the collaboration is over. Gathering this information is time-consuming, so remember this when you give them your rate for a project.

How Much Time?

After you know what they want you to do, you need to ask them when is the due date for the project. You have to know this for many reasons. You might blog full time but you do have a life outside of it. You might not be available to shoot a campaign if they are requesting it to be done in just a few days. You are going to have to plan all these out with others accordingly such as with a professional photographer if they request one.

Try not to have any collaborations that overlap each other. You should not post back-to-back collaborations on any social media. Sometimes it might happen with the brand sending their approval at the last minute, or the campaign timelines shifting.

Ask them if they want a draft and how soon they want it. At times, the brand might review the draft as soon as 48 hours. Other times, it might take them a month to send you revisions or approvals. Keep this in mind when planning your editorial calendar.

Do They Require Exclusivity?

Brands need to express all exclusive clauses up front. They might fail to mention one when you sign on to a campaign. They might place it in a tiny clause that you need a magnifying glass to read at the bottom of page eight of the contract. Exclusivity is something to consider if you blog in a certain niche. You might partner with beauty, travel, and fashion brands regularly. Any exclusivity period in any of these niches is going to interfere with your income.

If they do demand an exclusivity clause, you need to find out how long it is going to be and what retailers or categories need to be excluded. At times, an exclusivity clause might make you lose business. If you think an exclusivity clause is going to limit how many campaigns you will be able to take on, you can either negotiate it or ask for more money for the lost campaigns.

Are They Requesting Usage Rights?

This is the main thing bloggers fail to think about when taking on a campaign. Brands don't usually mention this when negotiating a deal and just slip it to you in the contract.

If you don't know how to ask this question, just say, "Are you requesting usage right for the content that is being produced in this campaign?" The brand might just want rights to repost any content on social media and you get the credit. This is pretty standard. If they start requesting a copyright, ownership, or photo license of your work, you need to renegotiate that part of the contract or ask for more money.

Is There a Budget? What are the Terms of Payment?

You have to always think about compensation. This is probably the first question a blogger asks a brand before beginning any collaboration. It is good advice to ask a lot of questions before sending them your rates. Each collaboration will be different. There will never be a one size fits all price tag for any collaboration. You can calculate your rate based on these factors: analytic reports, photo licenses, exclusivity clauses, turnaround time, the scope of work, and travel, if necessary.

Giveaways

You might have seen blogs that are constantly doing giveaways. You saw how popular they are and thought you should do the same.

If you are serious about investing in your blog but have not announced any giveaways, you are not doing the maximum for your marketing like you should be. If you think giveaways are not important to blogging, you are so wrong.

Giveaways and contests are two of the best techniques you can use to increase traffic to your blog. If you are a new blogger, contests can help you attract new readers. You just have to pick the correct product and then make sure you market the contest.

The main idea about these contests is that they will get you free advertising, free backlinks, and bring in new readers. The contest strategy always seems to work and is beneficial to new bloggers.

Backlinks

When running any contest, it doesn't matter if the prize is free cash, eBooks, software, or advertising. You are still going to attract new bloggers who in turn will advertise your contest on their site, giving you a backlink.

Since these bloggers give you a backlink, they are not just helping get more traffic to your blog, they are also building your authority. This helps you get even more traffic.

On the same line, if you see a contest and know without a shadow of a doubt that the blog is legitimate and trustworthy, share the information with your readers. This also increases your authority, credibility, and value.

Social Traffic

Even though you are getting traffic from backlinks, contests can help you promote your blog to new people who will then share your blog with their own followers.

You just add a specific condition in order for them to enter. For example, "To enter the contest, share on Instagram, Facebook, etc."

If you use this method right, you just might get a huge spike in traffic to your blog.

Since this traffic is coming from social media, it will be targeted a lot. This brings many benefits, including social proof.

Advertising

Along with free traffic and backlinks, contests will give you free advertising. Your blog is being exposed to a lot of other new blogs. As such, you will be able to directly appeal to the readers of these other blogs. This type of advertising and promotion is hard to come by.

You are going to generate new subscribers all for free with a giveaway or a contest. These new readers are going to start following your blog.

If you can run a successful contest, it will expose your brand to advertisers. These advertisers might want to sponsor your next contest.

Readers Get Rewards

If you have been wondering how you can thank your loyal readers, the answer is simple. Create a giveaway.

Reward your readers with giveaways. You need to be sure the prizes are useful and they will sufficiently reward your readers.

If you have a lot of readers and they are constantly supporting you, you have to reward them.

But this doesn't just reward your followers. It motivates them to actively support you more.

Increase Your Statistics

You might organize a giveaway where readers have to sign up for your email list. You might end up with 25 to 30 new subscribers. Some of those might end up unsubscribing but look at how many you gain overall.

Conclusion

Thank you for making it through the end of *How to Write a Blog*. I hope it was informative and that it was able to provide you with the tools you need to achieve your goals whatever they may be.

The next step is to take your blog to the next level. Start writing high-quality articles that will grow your following and make readers want to come back. It's not enough to just post articles that you want to write. You have to create articles that your readers want to read.

Finally, if you found this book useful in any way, a review on Amazon is always appreciated!

Blogging for Profit

The #1 Beginner's Guide to Earn $100+ for Day in 30 Days

(Only High-Profitable Online Marketing Strategies)

Table of Contents

Introduction

Let's start off with a strong dose of honesty here: this is probably not your first time trying to get the inside scoop on how money is made in the blogging world, is it? Chances are you have read several blog posts, downloaded a few freebies, and maybe even checked out a few other titles before landing here, on *Blogging for Profit*. The reality is that there are a lot of books out there on blogging and how you can use it to increase your income. Ever since the mid-2000s, when a handful of highly profitable Mommy bloggers popped up and shocked readers by how they were earning a healthy income just by sharing updates about their favorite recipes, crafts, and child-rearing tips, blogging has been put under the microscope. People are fascinated by the idea of being able to make money just by sharing their thoughts on things. Hence, why you can find about three million average-at-best guides out there to support you in getting started—this isn't one of them.

Blogging for profit is something that is still highly doable and that, when done right, can still earn you a major income. That being said, most of what you are hearing around the grapevine is outdated news. Finding the nitty-gritty on what it takes to launch an actual successful blog and really make a solid income off of it these days takes some effort, some research, and some straight up intention. So, rather than letting you wade through the hundreds of thousands of outdated posts that will give you the go around and keep you feeling overwhelmed, I have decided to create *the best blogging for profit book* **ever.**

Everything that you will learn in this guide is real, relevant, and recent. You will discover how you can seriously launch a blog and begin earning $100 every single day within your first 30 days on the scene. This guide is all about what it *really* takes to have a successful blog: marketing. That's right; you will learn how to manage a marketable blog that will become so successful, that soon you will be earning a phenomenal living from your blog by employing the *real* and *useful* tips from within this guide. So, if you are ready to begin, let's go!

Chapter 1: Do You Have What it Takes?

First things first: blogging is not for everybody. Yes, it is true that blogging is not hard. Posting at least once per week, sharing valuable content with your audience, and then strategically placing and marketing that content is about all it takes. However, not everyone is committed, devoted, or opinionated enough to really keep a blog going. Furthermore, there are a few extra things you have to do in the modern world to keep your blog afloat and really get it out there in front of your audience so that they don't just land on someone else's blog.

Having what it takes is not nearly as challenging as it sounds, but it does require you to be on your game and ready to invest at least a couple of hours per week into your blog. Once you have, you can begin earning a profit from it in no time flat. Throughout the rest of this chapter, we will address some common questions that most new or aspiring bloggers have. Make sure you pay attention because these answers are filled with gold. Not only will they give you advice on what to do and how, but they will also help you determine whether or not this is something you actually feel that you are ready and capable of doing.

Are You Passionate Enough?

Believe it or not, blogging does require a fair bit of passion. To put it simply, if you do not love what you are writing about, writing about it will be a challenge and will probably bore you to tears. Furthermore, you will probably not be invested enough to share about it in a way that your readers will actually be willing to read about. Your readers want someone who is so passionate about what they are writing about that they can genuinely feel you going the extra mile to bring value even when it is not necessarily a requirement. Furthermore, this passion will keep *you* easily committed to writing more. If you attempt to write about something you have a vague interest in or that is trending in your life this week, but that you are not truly passionate about, you will get bored fast. Your readers will pick up on that, and then, no matter how hard you try, marketing your content will be an uphill losing battle. Choose something you are passionate about. If there is nothing you feel passionate enough about that you could share on for a long time, this may not be the right move for you.

Will You Give A Unique Perspective?

I want to share something real with you, but not with the intention of scaring you off. That is, there are already writers in your desired niche. Some of those writers are good. *Really* good. If you want to get into blogging and succeed, you need to make sure that you are willing to compete with *them*. You should be willing to bring your own very unique perspective to the table. Do not try and copy someone who is already thriving in your niche, no matter how great they are doing. While learning from them by way of finding great areas to hang out and share your blog, and how to make your page look even more phenomenal is great, but attempting to directly copy their perspective will lose you followers. People might see you as a knock-off, or they would simply prefer to go to the person they already know and have a relationship with. Consider your own unique voice and build on that. Trust me, the more unique and *you* that you are, the more people will love following you.

How Do You Feel About Networking?

Building something like a blog requires you to be willing to network. In order to later convert your readers into consumers who purchase your products, you need people who genuinely care. They care about you by feeling like they have a relationship with you, which they gain through your networking abilities. Feeling confident in your ability to reach out to and connect with others is a great skill, as it will support you in sharing your blog, connecting with other bloggers so that you can collaborate and grow, and otherwise spreading the word about your blog.

Will You Dedicate to Learning?

Writing a blog is a long-term commitment. You can assume that the niche you are writing on will change, grow, or otherwise evolve over time. Being willing to stay on top of these things through learning is important. Furthermore, there is a learning curve that you need to settle into when it comes to launching a blog. Having the devotion to ensure that you are willing to continue learning as you get the hang of things is important. If you think you will just give up if you do not get it straight away, this may not be for you. While blogging is not hard, there are a few things you will need to really get to understand if you will make the most with your blog.

Can You Set (And Achieve) Goals?

Blogging does have many different goals that need to be set. These goals are generally personal to each blogger, but they are important nonetheless. A number of daily and monthly readers, income levels, and engagement are just a few things that bloggers generally like to incorporate into their goals to ensure that they are striving to move forward with their blog. Having the ability to set and achieve goals is a great skill to have as it will support you in staying committed to finding the best ways to reach and serve your audience with your blog.

Do You Plan On Staying Devoted Until You Succeed?

This guide is intended to get you to $100+ a day in as little as 30 days. If you apply these steps and stay focused all month long, you can feel confident that you will be turning a profit with your blog. However, if you fail to stay committed and you fall behind, give up, or stop applying _all_ of the advice within this book, you are severely hindering your chance to create that success. If you are not willing to stay devoted until you begin seeing results, blogging may not be for you.

Are You Willing To Do The Profitable Extras?

This question may be somewhat redundant because the reality is that anyone who is wanting to blog for profit is, of course, ready to do the extras. After all, these extras stand to make you a fairly large profit in the end! (And yes, blogging is still a highly profitable practice.) Writing a blog is simple: you write, you hit publish, and you carry on until you feel like writing again. Writing a blog *for profit* takes a few extra steps. You need to optimize your brand, network, market, and share your blog so that you get seen by readers. Then, you need to convert those readers into customers. This is the part that generally requires learning: you need to learn what your readers respond best to because this is what they are more likely to come back for. If they are more likely to come back, they are more likely to purchase. If they purchase and are kept satisfied, they are more likely to purchase again and share you with their friends. Staying devoted to doing the profitable extras will get you far, even earning a strong profit in minimal timing. However, it does require you to be willing to actually do those extras to create the profit.

Are You Ready?

The last thing you need to consider is if you are truly ready. If you have been browsing through the above questions and you are nodding to yourself and feeling confident, then there is a great chance that you are ready to begin blogging for profit. In that case, you should carry on to Chapter 2 and begin learning the ways that the standard blogger makes their income.

Chapter 2: Break Down of a Blogger's Income

Bloggers have several ways that they create an income through their blogs. Affiliate programs, guest posting, and display ads are some of the most commonly known ways. However, they are not often talked about in a way that truly supports beginners in understanding how to take full advantage of these advertisement opportunities.

If you truly want to generate a great income through your blog, you need to know the "behind the scenes" stuff that most bloggers do not want to openly share about on their pages because this would debunk the mystique that they keep up. It might also have a negative impact on how their current financial deals are going. So, consider this your official induction into the blogger locker room where you will learn about how these things *really* earn you money.

There are three ways that bloggers talk about most when it comes to making money: affiliate programs, guest posting, and advertisements. These three methods provide a great opportunity for bloggers to collaborate with other companies to create an income for themselves. Let's take a moment to explore each of these in-depth so that you can have a greater understanding of how these three methods work.

Affiliate Marketing

Affiliate marketing is a great marketing strategy that allows you to collaborate with companies who want exposure for their brands. Essentially, you blog about them and let your audience know about their products or services, and they pay you to do it. This is why you see many blogs with a disclaimer like: *"Products and services in this post may be sponsored through an affiliate program so that I can better serve you."* This disclaimer is not only a polite way to let their readers know that they may be profiting off of the post, but also it is a legal requirement. If you will be ranking on Google searches, you must have disclaimers on all of your affiliated or sponsored posts.

There are many ways that bloggers get started with affiliate marketing. Many programs like Amazon Affiliate and ClickBanks exist to support bloggers in finding these programs to join so that they can begin making an income from their blog. The nice thing about having a sponsorship program such as this is that it means you do not have to wait for companies to reach out to you to market for them. However, you need to be aware of how much you actually stand to make from these programs. For example, while Amazon Affiliate is a great starter program, you do not actually make a lot of money from them. So, while you can make *some*, if you are looking to hit $100+ days early on, this would not be a good starting point for you. Instead, consider a program that will offer you greater payouts for each referral you make.

Once you grow your audience a bit more, you can begin reaching out to companies and asking them if they would like to use you as an affiliate marketer. Alternatively, if you know of any companies that fit your niche that have built-in affiliate programs, you can apply for those as well. The more affiliate deals you are a part of, the more you stand to make, but it is important to make sure that you are nurturing each deal accordingly so that you can make funds from these deals!

Guest Posting

In the blogging world, guest posting means that you create a post for someone else's blog and they will host it for you. You can then create a post on your own blog that markets this post on their blog. Many bloggers who already have a thousand or more followers will begin offering these services, paid. Offering to guest post on someone else's blog is a great way to share your audience, as well as share your expertise with their readers. The idea here is that someone will pay you and you will write for them and then promote your writing on their blog to your own audience. This offers them the opportunity to market a unique piece of information to their audience, as well as access to your audience when you send your readers over.

While this will not necessarily be something you can do as a paid service with less than a thousand readers per month, or at least some form of established audience, it is still a great way to begin getting your audience larger. You can practice guest blogging early on as a way to expand your audience faster and then, once you have a more established audience, you can begin offering this as a service.

Advertisements

Paid advertisements are a great way to begin creating an income from your blog. On

Wordpress, there is a plugin you can use that will allow you to begin monetizing your blog through various paid advertisements. The most common way to do paid advertisements on a blog is through Google Ads. This plugin can easily be installed, and then you simply create an account with Google Ads and give them permission to advertise on your blog. You place specific areas on your blog where their advertisements will be shown and then every time someone clicks the ad, you are paid. This is called "pay per click."

Another way that bloggers will advertise on their page is by offering privately paid advertising packages. This allows companies with the same audience as you to pay you a fee per month and you display their ad (and their ad only) in certain places on your blogging website. These packages require more hands-on attention than Google Ads, but they do have the capacity to earn you more money per month, depending on the deal you create with the advertiser. However, these have become increasingly less common since the introduction of Affiliate Marketing, which tends to be more cost-effective for marketers.

These three primary ways ultimately make up the most common ways that virtually all bloggers create an income from their website. However, they are not the only ways available. This is just to give you a clear breakdown of where the bulk of most bloggers are earning from. In "Chapter 6: Converting Readers to Customers" we will explore even more options and give you an idea of how you can make even more cash through your blog.

Chapter 3: Blog Maintenance

Building and maintaining a blog is not entirely hard, but it does require you to give it at least a few hours per week. As you are building your blog, you will want to make sure that you focus on the things that matter most so that you do not end up wasting your time doing things that will not have a strong impact on your bottom line. In this chapter, we will discover what actually matters, how you can maintain it, and what is required on a week-to-week basis to make sure that you keep your blog well-maintained and profitable.

Building Your Brand

Your blog may only require your attention a few hours per week, but it still needs to have a strong brand if you will be able to increase your audience successfully and have the amount of reach that you desire to have. Building your brand for a blog that will make you $100+ per day within

30 days requires you to build an extremely strong brand. You should not be wasting your time with saying things like "I'll just start here and make it better later." No. You need to start out as the best. If you do not, people are not going to care, and there will be no reason for you to make it better. Starting strong requires you to invest in having strong branding. Fortunately, this does not have to be wildly expensive, nor does it have to be overly challenging, either.

Building your brand requires three things: your look, your tone, and your outreach. For your look, you need to have a logo, a color scheme, and a font package. You can find great inspiration online. The best way to make sure that you are creating an *excellent* blog is to check out the blogs owned by other people in your desired industry who are doing incredibly. Pay attention to what elements they use, how many, and how they go together. For example: do they use minimalistic colors with black, white, and one additional color?

155

Or are they more vibrant, incorporating a handful of bright colors together? Are their fonts playful and round, or are they straight and clean? Pay attention to things like this. The ones that are highly successful already have an idea of what image your reader is looking for. While you do not want to directly copy them (remember, this will not set you apart so readers will have no unique reason to read *your* content over anyone else's,) you do want to use this as an opportunity to learn about what your target market actually wants to see and then create something that will be visually appealing for them. As you are creating the elements of your blog through your branding package, make sure you include the color scheme, text package, a logo, a banner for your blog, and a template of the image that will represent each new blog post. You can also include Pinterest, Facebook, and Instagram graphic templates that go well with your brand and include your brand colors. Doing this will ensure that your brand looks uniform everywhere on the net.

Your tone is the next thing that matters. The way you present yourself through your online voice needs to stay consistent so that your audience knows what to expect with you. This way, they know if they relate to you or not. For example, Ree Drummond at Pioneer Woman has a very soft-spoken, family-oriented, traditional country tone. Gary Vee has a very to-the-point, no BS, clear tone. Wendy Nguyen has a very New York, fabulous fashion tone. Identifying your tone and keeping it uniform is important. This is your key communication method for your online personality. Your readers will want to know what to expect to read when they read your content. Will it be funny? Will it be on point? Will it fill them with memories of their childhood? Will it inspire them? Clarity and uniformity are important. This does not mean that you cannot be a serious writer who incorporates jokes from time to time. Rather, it means your overall image should remain serious if serious is the tone you are going for.

The way you reach out to engage with your audience is important, too. This is chosen both through marketing research and preference. The platforms you hang out on and reach out to your audience on the most say a lot about you and your brand. For example, if you are on Twitter, you can guarantee that both you and your readers are big fans of information fed in a short manner. This gives the illusion that you are direct and to the point, no matter what you are talking about. Twitter users tend to be more politically charged in one way or another since this tends to be the primary focus on the platform. If you are on Instagram, this means that you have a younger vibe to you and that you are passionate about sharing through sight. You likely prefer things to be tangible, and you want to bring this to your reader as well. For example, you do not just want to tell them about the new product you tried, you want to *show* them. Facebook is another great outreach platform because it incorporates image sharing, short posts, long posts, and article sharing all into one platform. While a younger audience will be less likely to follow you here, an older and more mature audience will love following you on Facebook. Pinterest is another great platform for bloggers. Interested folks (primarily women) flock to Pinterest to learn about everything from new recipes and DIY to parenting and relationship advice. Having an active Pinterest account is a great way to attract a bigger audience as well. Keeping yourself online and maximizing your outreach by hanging out in a few areas is important. You need to create your profiles and begin building and maintaining them as soon as you start your blog. This is how you will market new posts, stay engaged with your audience, and share dialogue with them in a more intimate way through commenting and messages that your blog itself does not allow for.

Proper Post Maintenance

Proper posting maintenance on your blog is important. You need to be posting at least once per week, sharing relevant and interesting content for your audience. This is a minimum. Most bloggers will post on average two or three times per week. There are two ways that you can accomplish this volume to make sure that you are posting regularly to keep new content coming out for your audience. One requires you to schedule an hour or two per week to write and market your writing, whereas the other requires you to set aside a few hours each month to write out a few posts and schedule them for your blog. Writing on a week-to-week basis tends to be a better way of keeping up with relevant trends, staying real-time with your audience, and keeping your own schedule more evenly distributed.

However, if you find that you are looking for a more flexible schedule, the monthly scheduling system may be more reasonable for you. It is important that you do not schedule out more than a month in advance, however, as you may then find yourself becoming irrelevant. In most niches, trends change so frequently that if you write about one and schedule it more than a couple of weeks out you may end up looking very behind-the-trend and thus people will be less likely to read your blog and more likely to read someone else's. If you do choose this schedule, make sure that you keep trends released very close to the date, or keep some flexibility so you can adjust your post schedule later to include more relevant trends as they arise.

Integrating External Platforms

Integrating external platforms into your blog is essential. This is how you will reach your audience and market to them. The three most important external platforms that you need to integrate with are an email marketing platform and at least one social media platform. On your blog, these can be integrated by installing a plugin, setting up your account or profile with the other platform, and then encouraging readers on your website to go over to those external platforms.

For email, the two best external sources to go to are AWeber and ClickFunnels. AWeber is a great all-around email marketing platform that will allow you to capture emails. That way, each week you can send out an email with updates and your latest blog post inside. Your readers can then open the email and head to your website to see what the latest post is all about. They say that having an email list is essential because if any social media platform was to ever go down, you would have no way of accessing your audience. Social media is consistently changing so while it is a great outreach, it is not guaranteed. Email is the only guaranteed point of contact on the internet, so it is essential that you start building your list.

ClickFunnels is another great platform. This one, however, will allow you to build a landing page and you can even incorporate sellable products or services into the page. For example, someone can give you their email in exchange for a free eBook, guide, list, recipe, pattern, DIY project, or other small gifts. Alternatively, you can use it to get their email in exchange for a small-priced item, such as a larger form of any of the aforementioned gifts. Ideally, your product or service should be $10 or less as this is a price point that most people barely think about. This way, you get your reader's emails, and you are able to make a small sale to them. So, at the same time as capturing their contact information for marketing, you are converting them into customers. ClickFunnels does cost a bit more per month, but their service is highly reliable, easy to use, and makes creating funnels extremely simple for beginners.

Facebook is another important outreach point. Some people will choose to bypass Facebook and land on different social media platforms. While you do not have to abandon all other social media in favor of Facebook, having Facebook incorporated is important. First and foremost,

Facebook offers integration features for most blogs that will support you in bringing your audience over to a social media platform. No matter how young or old your audience is, most have Facebook, so this is a great catch-all for your readers. Then, Facebook offers many great marketing features. From having your own page where you share updates about your latest blog posts and exclusive happenings in your life, to having messenger-based marketing features and more. Facebook offers many great ways to get in touch with your audience. Plus, you can then transport them from Facebook over to their chosen social media platform where you *also* hang out. That way, you capture your audience on social media as well. The more they follow you and are connected with you, the easier it is for you to be seen by them and thus the better your chances are at making a greater living off of your blog since your return-reader-ratio will be higher.

Chapter 4: Wordpress

Creating your blog is essential. There are many Wordpress.com technical guides out there that will support you in creating your blog, but few are really designed to help you optimize your blog from a marketing front. That being said, if your blog is not optimized from a marketing standpoint, you are not going to have the best chances at retaining readers and converting them into customers. You *need* to consider the marketability of your blog website. In this chapter, we will optimize your blog so that readers are not only captivated by your page the first time they land on it, but they are inspired to follow you, bookmark you, and look for you on other platforms so they can stay up-to-date with all of the great content you share.

Your Template

The first part of having a strong, marketable blog is making sure that you are using the right template. On Wordpress, there are hundreds of templates to choose from. If you do not find what you love on their website, you can do a Google search and find many other third-party companies who build Wordpress templates that you can install and upload to your blog.

When you are choosing a template, there are a few things that you need to look for. First, you need to make sure that the template actually matches the look of your brand. You do not want to have a minimalist brand using a retro template, or a modern restaurant using a traditional theme. Pay attention to the look and make sure that you can genuinely see your own personal brand matching with it well.

Next, you need to consider functionality. The template you choose should make it easy for readers to locate everything. There should also be a spot where you can easily put a call to action in place that will draw your readers out to your email capturing service and your social media pages. If there is not one built into the template, make sure you can easily envision where one would go and that it would genuinely look as though it fits in and not like it was sloppily tossed in after the fact.

Lastly, you need to choose a template that is mobile ready. Most of your readers will be reading you from their phone. A shrinking number of people visit your site from a desktop, so while you want to make sure that you are desktop compatible as well, keeping your page mobile-friendly is important. Any blogs that are not optimized for mobile devices are quickly skipped over in favor of ones that are. Do not forget to check what the template looks like on mobile and make sure that all of the features are still functional, easy to see, and easy to read so that your reader can enjoy your blog.

Incorporating Your Brand

As you optimize your Wordpress blog, make sure that you are incorporating your brand into it. In the "Personalization" tab you can find many different customizations you can make. Specific customizations that are available will depend based on what theme you have chosen. Double check each of these to make sure that they incorporate your brand color, text, and design. This will keep your page looking uniform and will make sure that people can easily identify you. Take some time to really focus on making sure that your brand integrates in a way that is stunning. Simply throwing your colors on the template is not enough. Consider which highlight and base colors you will use and how they fit into your template to make sure that they look amazing. People are a lot pickier about this these days, so make sure you are catering to their need to be visually enticed so that they are more eager to stick around.

Your branding on your Wordpress page is like your storefront. If it looks attractive and enjoyable, people will be more likely to bookmark you and come back. If it looks mediocre, they will take what they need, but they probably will not come back. If it looks any less than that, they will probably find a new page altogether to find the information that they are looking for.

Keeping It Simple

Your website should be easy to understand. Many people like to look at their page as a flowing process. Your new or potential reader should land on your page and know exactly what to do and where to go. Ideally, the first place they should look is your blog. Then, when they become interested in you, they will click over to your about page. There, they should be introduced to all of what you do. So, if you have a store or a brand that actually sells things (courses, handmade products, etc.) this should be discussed in your "About Me" page because then they will be more likely to head over to see what you have available.

For your call to action that captures their email, you should have this simple as well. Keep it in an easy-to-access spot that exists on all of the main pages so that when your new visitor becomes interested, they can input their email to receive their freebie and get more information about your blog and your brand. Ideally, you should also include a delayed pop up that allows your new visitor to input their email. That way if they forget to do it whilst on the pages they are visiting, they are prompted to do it before they leave. Make sure that the pop up is able to be exited by your visitor in case they do not want to give you their email. Pop-ups that cannot be exited are actually considered spam and can result in your page not ranking. Furthermore, Wordpress does not allow them.

Your External Integration Features

Make sure that all of your external integration features are set up properly. The last thing you want is for someone to go to input their email and be drawn to a broken link or taken to a ClickFunnel or AWeber site that is not yours. Double check everything you create to make sure it works properly. Ideally, you should navigate your blog as though you are a visitor and test each feature as such as well. This will ensure that you are keeping your links optimized and that all of the features work properly.

Optimizing Your Posts

Posts are ultimately the reason why people are landing on your page. People want to read what you have to say! That is the entire point of a blog, after all. Keeping your blog posts optimized can ensure that people find exactly what they are looking for, that each post is professional and easy to read, and that you present yourself in a manner that suggests you care. People who do not take the time to optimize their posts ultimately get seen as phony or as someone who does not care enough to check, this results in you having your readers go somewhere else—to a person who does check and keep their posts optimized and professional looking.

To do this, make sure that you check for grammar and any spelling errors and fix them. You should also ensure that all links within your posts are optimized to keep the information or products and services that you are referring to easy to access by your audience. Keep your paragraphs short and clean, so it is easier for your audience to read. Long, drawn-out paragraphs are exhausting and overwhelming to look at, and will often result in your audience being disinterested in your content merely based on the look of it. Check your pictures to make sure that they are sized properly and that they look correct on both your desktop browser and your mobile browser. You can also make sure that they are high quality, so there is no blurriness or color distortion. Lastly, choose a highlight photo that is properly branded, sized, and designed so that each of your posts looks attractive to your readers. Remember, you really want to appeal to their visual eye.

As long as you take these considerations into mind when building your Wordpress site, you can feel confident that you are creating a strong page. Ultimately, the end goal is to analyze every single aspect of your page and make sure that it looks amazing for your audience. The better it looks, the better chances you have at having your audience fall in love with your page, remain long-time readers and follow you elsewhere on the net.

Chapter 5: Topping the Charts

Part of having a successful blog is knowing how to get to the top of Google charts and other search engine charts. With so many blogs on the web right now, being the best of the best is essential. This is how you get discovered, and this is how you make money. While this may sound challenging, it is actually quite simple. The main reason why most bloggers will not actually top the charts and go big is that they lack the necessary commitment to get there. As long as you stay focused and devoted, you are certain to make the top of the charts and to get yourself far more exposure for your ideal audience.

Getting to the Top of Search Engine Results

If you want to get seen, you need to get your blog to the top of search engine results. This is not as hard as it sounds, as long as you follow a few important steps. They are as follows:

1. *Write Great Quality Content*

    The better your quality, the better your results. When search engines "crawl" your pages to find information and present it to their searchers, they check to make sure that grammar and other such things are correct. They also want to make sure that what you are sharing is relevant to what the person is searching for. You can do this by writing great quality content that is popular and trending. Well-written blogs will naturally move up rankings as more visitors land on them, link to them, share them, and revisit them.

2. *Use Your Writing To Optimize Your Page*

    Search engines cannot see how pretty your page is. The aesthetics are for your readers. What a search engine is looking for is relevancy. They want to make sure that what you are sharing is aligned with what their user is looking for. They have bots known as "crawlers" that read the first one-third of each page before moving on to read the next page. This is how they produce their results. The ones that are most relevant are at the top of the search ranking. If your first one-third includes relevant keywords and information that relates to the search, you will be more likely to rank higher. Keep these words specific, relevant, and optimized for what your reader is most likely to search. For example, if they are looking for "easy recipes" your text should say "easy recipes" at least once in the first one-third of your post.

3. *Keywords In Text, Phrases, and Code*
   In addition to the first one-third of your page, your website, in general, should

contain keywords throughout. Your titles, phrases, texts, and even the names of the documents you upload and the code you input into your website should feature keywords relevant to your niche. This increases your relevancy and makes you more likely to be shown at the top of the list.

4. *Include External Links*

Sharing to reputable external links is another great way to get seen by your audience by rising up the list. Search engines love seeing this on pages because this means that you are increasing your user's experience by sharing high quality, reputable content with them. You can do this by sharing the link in your posts, or by having a directory of your favorite blogs and resources on your page.

5. *Share to Social Media*

Sharing your content on social media tells search engines that it is more relevant. Furthermore, it increases the number of people likely to visit your page—meaning your page hit number increases. As this number rises, search engines believe your page is more popular, so it is more likely to share it over other pages that are not too popular.

What Constitutes as "Quality" Content?

You may be wondering: what constitutes the high-quality content that search engines are looking for? The answer to this is quite simple. Furthermore, it is not necessarily the *direct* thing that search engines are looking for. Search engines do not have a brain; therefore, they are not capable of determining what content is interesting versus what content is not. What they are actually looking for is how many people have landed on your page. The more interesting and high-quality your content is, the more likely people will visit your website. Then, as your hit counter rises, your popularity rating rises in the back-end information that search engines are looking for.

Keeping quality content on your page is more about increasing your likelihood of being shared on other pages, websites, and social media accounts. It also increases your likelihood of being revisited by the same readers. So, when you are writing, you want to write things that are interesting, fresh, and relevant. The better it is written and the more it entices your readers, the more your rankings will naturally rise as you are shared amongst others.

There are several types of blog posts that are known to be considered more interesting by readers. The following templates are great ones to follow if you need inspiration on what constitutes as interesting and high quality to your readers.

Remember, grammatically correct writing that is free of spelling errors is important, too.

1. Tutorials and how-to guides
2. The latest industry-specific news and current events
3. Subjects that are considered controversial
4. Checklists (i.e., "New Baby Checklist," "New Home Checklist," "Spring Cleaning Checklist."
5. Lists (i.e., "5 Things You Need to Do Before Summer is Over."
6. Infographics
7. Case studies
8. Profiles on people relevant to your industry
9. Interviews
10. Expert advice
11. Comparisons and reviews
12. Video and audio content
13. Resources

14. Problems and solutions (i.e., "The One Thing You Need to Stop _____!")

15. What Others Are Saying (i.e., "What Gary Vee Thinks About _____ and Why I [Agree/Disagree.])

16. Behind-the-scenes content

17. Inspirational stories

18. Parody or funny posts

19. Quizzes, surveys, and polls

20. FAQs

21. Questions you should be asking (i.e., "Six Questions to Ask Before Hiring A Lawyer.")

22. Roundup posts (i.e., "The Top 10 Funniest Twitter Posts This Week" or "The Best Summer Wardrobe Pieces for 2019.")

23. Contests

24. Time-saving posts (i.e., "How to Save Time Buying Groceries.")

25. Event summaries

26. My top Takes on _____.

27. Rants

28. Beginner's guides

29. Guest bloggers

30. Myth vs. Fact posts

How Facebook Will Maximize Your Exposure

As you learned earlier in this chapter, sharing your content on social media is important. First, it shows search engines that your content is being shared, thus making it more "popular" in rankings and helping it rise to the top of the charts. Second, it helps it get seen by your target audience. This means that by sharing it with your building audience on Facebook, they are more likely to see it and click over to reading it. This behavior increases your hit counter, rising your content even further up the rankings. Another thing that happens is that it is more likely to be shared. Readers are more likely to share a post that is already made than they are to make their own post. So, having this part already done for them makes it far easier for your reader to tap "share" and show it to their own friends and family. The more it is shared, the more it rises up the ranks in search engines. Furthermore, the more it is seen by others, which means the more hit counts you get, the more likely you are to be shared again, and the higher you rise once more.

Another way that you can use Facebook is by creating a group. Building an online community is a great way to increase your outreach, thus giving you direct people to share your posts with. Furthermore, individuals in a group are more likely to engage than page followers. They are also more likely to see what you are sharing, based on the Facebook algorithm, giving them a better chance to actually see it. This means that building your community can have a great impact on helping you have a greater outreach. Lastly, Facebook groups are a community that you can pay attention to and listen inside of. As your group members begin engaging with you and each other, you can see what questions they are asking, what information they are searching for, and what they are sharing with each other. This makes it easier for you to determine what your target audience finds relevant and what you should be writing for future posts. Thus, Facebook groups are both a way to engage with and build loyalty amongst your existing readers and create relevant content to keep your current readers satisfied and attract new readers into your community.

Chapter 6: Converting Readers to Customers

Now that you have a strong idea of how you can create a powerfully marketable blog that is sure to attract an audience, it is time to learn how you can turn that audience into paying customers! This is ultimately how you will turn your blog into a highly profitable source of income for you. When done right, you will rapidly move beyond the $100+ per day target and into $250+ per day and beyond!

There are many ways that a blog can be monetized beyond the three most commonly discussed strategies that we discussed in Chapter 2. The strategies that will follow in this chapter are how bloggers are going from making pennies per month, to making a real income from their blog. There are many different strategies that you can use, and you are not required to use every single one to monetize your blog. That being said, you certainly could use them all if you so desired.

Direct Sales

Many people are involved in the direct sales industry. It also happens to be well-known for the number of people who are millionaires, thanks to the industry. If you want to maximize your income, getting into direct sales may be the best way to do it. Direct sales are not challenging, but they do require consistency. Unlike multi-level marketing (MLM) systems, you are not required to have a downline or to structure your genealogy tree in any particular way to maximize your income. Instead, you make money on all of the sales made through your channels, as well as you make a percentage off of everyone who signs under you. This makes it an extremely simple process, as well as straightforward and effortless to maintain.

Direct sales work similarly to affiliate marketing. You will still want to use a disclaimer—letting your readers know that you are profiting off of the products or services that you are recommending. Then, you can go ahead and write about them. Since you are using and reusing the same products or services over and over again with direct sales, you want to make sure that you write about them frequently. A great way to do this is to consider many different angles of how the product or service is impacting your life and how it could help others as well. For example, say that you are selling food products for a direct sales company. You could discuss the many different recipes that you are using these products and tools with, including ones that might be considered "classic" or "easy to find" (as these will draw attention to your page initially,) and ones that are unusual or different, yet still delicious. That way, if someone were to search up something simple like "meatloaf" they would find your page. However, they would see in the "related" section many other simple recipes made using the products your company sells that are not something they would typically look up. This creates an interesting and intrigue factor that encourages them to wander around your website more, thus increasing your popularity, your likelihood to be shared, and your profitability if they choose to order through your company from your channel.

Another great thing about direct sales is that you can create a system where, when people sign up underneath you, you coach them on how they can create a healthy profit as well. This could include something simple like a Facebook group where your downline consultants go to receive weekly coaching calls from you, as well as some free printables, handouts, guides, checklists, or anything else to keep them going. Since you make money off of the money they make, this increases your profitability. Furthermore, you increase your reach to their audience as they can then show their customers to your blog for inspiration and you can make cash by marketing other products to them through alternative affiliate links.

When you get into direct sales as a way to maximize your profit through your blog, make sure that you pay attention to the rules and fine print within the agreement. Not all companies are entirely flexible for bloggers. Some common problems bloggers run into when attempting to market with direct sales companies include rules that prevent them from discussing any other industry-specific products on the same blog as they are discussing the direct sales products on. Another one that some direct sales companies have is that if your blog exceeds a certain number of monthly viewers, you are not allowed to discuss the company any longer because it is deemed unfair to other sellers. These types of rules can inhibit your ability to market for these products or any other ones, so it is important that you pay attention. Do your best to find one that is flexible, high quality, and worthy of sharing with others. Also, do not share something that you yourself are not passionate about or willing to actively use. Your audience will know that you are being dishonest if they try the products and do not find them to be anything near what you are claiming.

Being honest and transparent is essential in retaining reader loyalty so that they are more likely to purchase from you.

Email Marketing

Email marketing is one of the longest-standing online marketing strategies that exists. It is a great system that gets you directly in front of your audience, and it also gives you the opportunity to withstand any changes in the algorithms to social media. While your posting visibility and the way posting on social media changes frequently as new trends arise, email marketing has virtually never changed. Simply join a platform like AWeber, capture emails, and begin marketing!

Capturing emails with a third-party application is simple. However, you have to give your audience a reason to want to give you their email. Most viewers will not be of the frame of mind where they simply want to give it to stay up-to-date. These days are long gone. Nowadays, readers will provide you with their email if you have something for them: a reason for them to do it that exceeds simply being able to be reminded to come back to your blog every so often. These are called "freebies." Freebies are typically generated around lists, checklists, guides, eBooks, automatic downloads, an exclusive course access, access to a private Facebook community, or anything else that your audience would want to have. It is important that you choose a freebie that they will actually want; as this will ensure that they are truly encouraged to exchange their email for the freebie. Choosing a freebie that is irrelevant will not be useful for you.

The best way to pick a freebie that will work is to pay attention to your target audience and answer these three questions:

1) What information do they want?
2) How do they like to consume information?

3) How much do they need to receive to be called into action?

By knowing what information they want and how they like to consume that information, you can get a strong idea of what the freebie itself should be. Then, you need to know how much of that information they would need to do something about it. While you do not want to be giving away anything huge that could easily be monetized, you also do not want to be creating a bland, basic freebie that they walk away from feeling like they gained no value from. Finding that happy medium is important.

When it comes to email marketing, there are many ways that you can get in touch with your audience and give them a reason to open your email. Ideally, you should email them once per week, maybe twice. As a beginner blogger, you do not want to overwhelm yourself. You also do not have the type of brand power that larger companies have that compels their audience to open daily emails. So, once or twice per week is plenty. In those emails, you should always include your latest post, even if you included it in the previous email (such as if you are emailing twice per week but only posting once).

You can also market directly within the email. For example, you can say something like "Plus, check out this great _____ I used in the post! Grab your own here and make _____ alongside me!" and place an affiliate link directly within the email. If you do this, once again make sure that you include a disclaimer at the bottom of the email. You can also make emails that are roundup style emails. For example "Check out all of my favorite Fall recipes from last year!" Since you already have plenty published, this will help your audience see everything that you have already done and had a great list compiled, to begin with. Furthermore, you get to profit off of recycling content. Any affiliate links that you have in these blog posts that are still usable will be exposed to your audience once more, thus increasing your profitability. For that reason, however, you should also make sure to take a browse through these older posts and refresh any as needed. That way you do not accidentally send out an email with posts that contain broken our outdated links that no longer work.

You should always make sure that when you send out an email, there is an opportunity for your subscribers to unsubscribe. Though you may not want them to, having an email without any unsubscribe options is actually illegal in most places. It goes against spam laws, which can result in you personally being held liable for the emails being sent that your readers cannot unsubscribe to. When you use companies like AWeber, these features are already built-in. However, if you attempt to do your own list without the assistance of a third-party platform, you will need to create this feature on your own.

Funnels

Creating sales funnels is a great way to create an income from your blog. Sales funnels are simple, and they have a major impact on converting your audience from readers to customers when built properly. ClickFunnels is a great service to use because they lay the entire process out for you and walk you through it step-by-step as they do all of the difficult work and you simply click your funnel into place.

Funnels are used as a way to get a reader to purchase a small product, which then leads them to a larger product that finally leads them to your largest product, which would be considered your best offer. For example, if you were a self-help blogger, you could start your funnel with an inexpensive $10-or-less eBook offer. Then, you would offer your readers an even more interesting offer: an instant download course worth $150+ that they receive for less than $50. Then, you would move on to offering them a consult call or a one-hour coaching call that would be worth $99. From there, you would pitch your client with a service that would suit their needs based on what you learned in that call.

Of course, this funnel is not exactly what all funnels need to look like. If you are not a coach, or you only sell products and not services, or anything else like that, you would adjust this funnel to accommodate for what you are actually offering. Furthermore, you are not required to stay in the $10, $50, and $99 price range. Instead, you can price it however you want. The idea when it comes to pricing is to start with something that is paid but is so inexpensive that they do not have to think twice about it. Research shows that anything under $50 typically does not require a lot of thought before purchasing when it comes to consumers. More often than not, they will just go ahead and purchase it. This initial offer shows the quality of your work and supports your new customer in seeing how much value you bring to the table and how much you can offer them.

The next offer they are given should be more expensive, but not as expensive as your final offer. This offer should be just as high quality, just as lucrative and desirable, and offered in a short time frame after they purchased the first item so that you fall into the window of opportunity where you are still fresh in their mind, and the content you are teaching is still interesting and worthwhile to them.

The second offer will lead to the third offer which is much larger and should initiate them into your final offer. If you are only offering products, this might actually be your final offer itself. If you are offering services, however, this should be the point where they convert from purchasing products to purchasing your time so they can get on a call with you. This would then give you the opportunity to make an official pitch face-to-face that would lead them into the next part of the process.

Funnels can either be time-consuming and require a lot from you, or they can be fully automated, and they require absolutely nothing from you. If you pre-record everything and produce products that hold their value and are never required to be changed (called "evergreen products,"), you can easily automate the entire thing, and you would never have to change anything because the products would do all of the work for you. In this case, your funnel would become a great source of passive income.

Memberships and Subscriptions

Memberships are a great way to monetize your blog. Many people who offer some form of service or have something that they can offer in addition to writing on an ongoing basis love making memberships or subscription services that will create an income for them. These are wonderful because with a membership or subscription service, you are only required to make one thing, and it serves your entire paid audience. For example, say you are a food blogger. Members or subscribers could pay a monthly fee to receive access to your exclusive recipes, exclusive discounts from various companies you are affiliated with, and other similar exclusive offers. If you are a coach blogging about self-help, this membership could feature one monthly weekend course that they could accomplish, plus one live training call hosted in an exclusive Facebook group only available to paying members.

Not all styles of blogs will work well with memberships or subscription services, but there are many unique styles that you can consider if you want to incorporate something like this into your blog. While these do take more time to nurture and keep going, they can also produce you a great income. If you are interested in doing something like this, you will need to consider a service or product that your audience would want to receive on a monthly basis (or whatever the term of your membership or subscription periods are.) Then, you would need to be willing to ensure that you produce the aforementioned product or service as promised every single month. However, if you are willing to commit to this, many bloggers make several thousands of dollars off of these services on a monthly basis. Plus, you do not need to have a large following to get started: all you need is one or two subscribers willing to commit, and from there it will continue to grow!

Courses, Products, and Services

Of course, selling courses, products, or services based on your blog's particular niche is a great way of increasing the amount of money that you make through your blog. These will take you time to produce, but they can give you something tangible to put in the hands of your audience in exchange for an income. This is one way that many bloggers build on their blog to create an even bigger income through their platform. When done right, it does not have to be challenging or all that time-consuming, either.

Courses tend to be the least time-consuming of all when it comes to choosing an option of how you can produce money on your blog. If you have a studio or a quiet office you can go to, you can easily videotape yourself as you share information that can then be turned into a video course. If you then add a few downloadable PDF files that offer written information and interactive guides or journals, you have a full course! These courses range in price from $15 - $1000+ depending on the length, the content itself, and the demand. You can easily create a handful of courses and offer them on your blog for a fee. Then, you simply market these courses alongside marketing your blog and every time someone signs up for one, you are paid for it!

People make courses for all types of reasons. In the blogosphere right now, there are courses that range in topics from how to cook to how to teach a cat to walk on a leash. People are interested in learning about so many different things, and this is great for you. For you, this means that you have the opportunity to create anything that appeals to your niche and market it for extra, passive income.

Products range in how demanding they are to provide. For simple products, such as instant-downloads and digital content, they may be less time-consuming. For handmade products, they may take a long time to create. You can also consider drop shipping, which is not as common with blogs, but it can certainly work to produce you more income without any interaction with the product itself. Typically, one of the easiest ways to provide products if you are not interested in making your own, however, are through direct sales and affiliate marketing.

When you sell products, you do incur more fees as a result of shipping expenses, time to make the products, and overhead. However, many people love purchasing products from their favorite bloggers. That is why famous bloggers such as Ree Drummond the Pioneer Woman have their own product lines. If you build up a following and you offer products that they would love to have, you can easily produce a higher income through this strategy.

Services are another time-consuming choice, but you are paid directly for your time. The most common services that offered are forms of coaching, consulting, counseling, or other similar services. However, you can also offer writing services, graphic design services, editing services, virtual assistant services, and other similar things. The services you offer will ultimately depend on what you are capable of providing your client with.

The best part about services is that you are not required to create something and then push to sell it. When it comes to creating things like handmade products, not only do you have to put the time into making it but you also have to wait for it to sell before you earn a profit. This means that you put in a lot of work without any guarantee of making a return on your time and resource investment. When it comes to services, you simply make a great offer and market it. You do not actually do any work until you are already paid for the service. This means that you do not invest so much time into something that is not necessarily guaranteed.

Social Media Communities

Social media communities will not necessarily make you money themselves, but they do increase your ability to convert readers into paying customers. With a social media community, such as a Facebook group, it creates the perfect environment for you to create a more intimate relationship with the people in your community.

Unlike fans of your profiles and pages, members of a group feel more intimately connected to you by the very nature of a group. Furthermore, it gives a sense of exclusivity and closeness with you. Creating a group to host a community and partaking in that community also gives you the opportunity to connect more with your biggest fans and followers. This means that you can engage with them in a more personalized way, thus earning even more loyalty from them. As you do this, they become more interested in purchasing your products, services, direct sales offers, and anything else you have available. So, while your community itself will not make you any money, the connections you create within that community maximize people's likelihood of purchasing your offers.

If you choose to do this, it is important that you spend your time genuinely cultivating a community. If people join your group only to realize that the only reason you have the group is so that you can constantly market to them, they are likely not going to stick around. Instead, spend time offering even more value and content within the group. Then, every so often you can share a marketing post. That way, people get to know you and like you through the group and when you do share something for them to purchase they are more likely to because they feel that you genuinely care and you are offering something that they would actually like, want, or need.

Conclusion

Congratulations on completing *Blogging for Profit!* I hope this book has lived up to your expectations by offering you real, unique, and powerful insight into the many ways that you can develop an income with your blog. By enforcing the strategies within this book, you can easily launch your own profitable blog that will earn you at least $100+ per day within the first 30 days.

In this book, you learned amazing and honest perspectives on how money can be made in the blogging world. Some require more time, some require less. The specific strategy you use will likely be a mixture of those offered in this book, perfectly blended in a way that allows you to be as hands-on or hands-off as you desire.

To summarize, here is what you need to do to have a successful blog that will help you earn a great profit:

1. *Create a brand that is not just good but excellent, and make it easily identifiable*
2. *Design your Wordpress blog to be attractive and search engine optimized*
3. *Share your blog frequently across multiple platforms to expand your exposure*
4. *Create a profitable feature that will maximize your income (i.e., affiliate marketing, products or services, a funnel...)*
5. *Earn $100+ per day!*

Creating a blog is not challenging, but it does require a specific attention to detail and style to really get yourself out in front of your audience and recognized. Remember, there are many bloggers on the scene, but there are not many *amazing* bloggers. As long as you stay devoted and you commit to being the best, you have already moved far up above most other bloggers out there. By staying focused and keeping yourself on track, you can guarantee your success. With that, $100+ per day will be just the start for you. From there, you will definitely go far above and beyond where you will begin earning way more money! If you are looking to expand even further, you should definitely check out my second book: *How to Make Money Blogging: The #1 Advanced Guide to Earn $250+ for Day in 90 Days with Search Engine Optimization Monetizable Techniques (Zero-Cost Online Marketing Strategy)*! This book would be the perfect next step for you in going even further with your blog and increasing your income from it.

Lastly, if you enjoyed reading *Blogging for Profit* and felt that it provided plenty of value for you in your venture to create a strong profit from your blog, please take a moment to review it on Amazon Kindle. Your honest feedback would be greatly appreciated.

How To Make Money Blogging

The #1 Advanced Guide to Earn $250+ For Day in 90 Days with Search Engine Optimization Monetizable Techniques (Zero-Cost Online Marketing Strategy)

Table of Contents

Introduction

In today's fast developing online industry, it is very difficult to avoid getting into blogging about something or the other. We are so used to seeing celebrities taking advantage of having an online presence, so why not the average person?

There is nothing to stop anyone from setting up a blog purely to earn money and have a healthy interest in writing and promoting it. In this e-book, we are going to take a thorough look at ways to incorporate blogging into your business and also earn money from a personal blog. This e-book will show you how to launch and expand a business through the medium of digital marketing, so you work smart and learn something too.

Chapter 1: What Is SEO?

SEO (Search Engine Optimization) do you really know what the term means, and should you care about it if you have a blog that needs to be earning an income for you? These days blogging is a popular way to get before a global audience without breaking the bank, in this e-book we are going to look at what SEO can do for your online presence, the rationale of it and, how to use it your advantage, and also elude methods that could get your account blocked.

The phrase Search Engine Optimization (SEO) explains the route that affects your blog's status, in the blogosphere, i.e., the place it has on the ranking page when some writes in a search term.

For example, if you have a cake decorating business, and you also run a blog about the subject, when someone wants to order a fancy cake, your blog has to be optimized so that when someone writes in 'where to buy fancy cakes locally' into Google search bar your blog should appear on page one of the search results at the number one spot. Keep in mind that Google is the largest and most used search engine in the world to locate services and businesses.

This imperative because it all about getting visitors to your blog so they can see what you are selling. You can always buy in traffic from a local web company to grow your customer base but don't do it till you know what you are paying for. The great the traffic that comes to your blog, the better the opportunities that you will make sales. You want to make sure that you never leave the number one spot on page number one because you will get as much sixty percent of the clicks. Make sure that all your pages are up to speed because Google grades singular site pages rather than complete blogs. Google sends robots to your page, and they follow orders!

Whether you are running a personal blog or a business one, Google have an everchanging methodology or algorithm to ascertain the relevance of a page. Although Google can be quite transparent about sharing information as how it comes to a decision, much of it is shrouded in mystery, because they really don't want to share that kind of information in case people abuse it. All you need to know is how search engines work and to make sure they work to your advantage.

Your blog has to be relevant to what your message is all about. People come to search engines to look for something. It could be information, or they are looking to purchase an item. This next point is very important, make sure at all times that the methods you use to monetize your blogs are genuine and honest, because you don't want to be banned from Google. Trust is a very high issue with Google and almost impossible to get reinstated

Here we need to consider some important things that can tell you if your site is search engine friendly. Here is a checklist of things.

On-site SEO

It must have original and applicable information. All your copy has to be highly fixated on the topic of 'fancy cakes,' and the long tail keywords and keywords, in general, should be concentrated on that only. These days you don't have to cram in keywords you can be more selective in how you place them on your blog. This is what you should have the URL your blog's name/ "fancy-cakes-shop- in- San Diego," the page title (H1 tag), yes that choice of words would represent about 1.5% of the copy on that page.

Closed Site Seo

Most sites have backlinks coming back to them and for Search Engine Optimization recognition.

You can obtain backlinks by, writing observations or short content on those sites that include a connection to your site. Wait till you know what you are doing because the need to make sure that they relevant to your niche and target market which is the local area. As you get into the whole realm of blogging, you will discover many new techniques most of them are usually free.

Utilize Promotional Websites

A big kudos for many bloggers is that the Internet has a disparate plethora of platforms and sites that can be used both for personal opinions and commercial requirements. Some are funded platforms selling advertisement spaces, PPC, and blogging sites through quantified spheres.

Ambitious personal bloggers as well as commercial blog owners who wish to have a steadfast growth of their blog activity. Picking just one platform that can do the job for them should suffice in the beginning. Bloggers would have to remember that the platforms have limitations and only access a limited client base and that they need to have wide portfolio to bring in fresh clients.

Socializing Is Important

Due to the wealth of social networking sites, you can generate a huge following, but they need to be the right group and, if cultivated right, can become the backbone in almost any promotional campaign online. Social networking sites enable blog owners to fluidly and easily communicate with their existing clients. These sites personalize the company whereby clients are able to relate to a real person and discuss ideas and influence future product packages.

Apart from that, social networking sites work as greatly as its offline counterpart through referrals.

Chapter 2: Choosing the Right Name and Keyword

A blog with informative and well-written articles will definitely get into Google's and other search engines good books. Learning how to start a blog is easy, but it is the next part that requires skills, passion, and dedication. Your blog needs to be a good and enduring supply of fresh content and being an obsessive writer could make an authority within your field. A profitable site is continuously advancing, and your content is being curated by Google through algorithm's all of the time.

Scheduling your blog posts

When planning your blog content writing for your new online business, it can be difficult to come up with fresh new ideas. To develop an influential blog that resounds of authority, and attracts many visitors you need to be updating it consistently and habitually. This can be done by planning and organizing your posts through a schedule. You have probably come from that regimented environment where there has been rigorous scheduling and time management. This same regimen also applies to when you are writing a blog the only difference is that now you are working from home. So, you are groaning, but once the schedule is set up for your blog content writing and put into place, you'll realize how much easier it is to work.

Go ahead with the first task of deciding on a time for your blogging calendar. When you set up your first blog calendar choose a shorter period of a month or even a quarter.

Then formulate a list of topics that you want to discuss in your blog posts. When you are thinking of ideas here, put yourself in the shoes of your target audience and write on issues they might be keen to know about.

Right, now that is behind you time to do keyword research to find out what phrases related to those topics are being searched. Source out phrases which are being searched and which have a low competition for you to have a chance of competing against.

Now pick the days when you will be publishing a blog post and record those on a calendar. Next, to each entry write in the title, the keyword phrase you will focus on, and a short summary of the topic you will write about.

To set up this schedule some outlay of your time will be necessary, but once you have done it, you will find that you get blog posts published more regularly and efficiently. When the time comes to write your blog post for that day, all the planning and preparation has been done, and all you need to do is write it out, it's that simple. Also, you are creating a log of ideas, and that is a good thing because you won't miss anything.

Managing and monetizing a blog is a big project, so if you break it into smaller more manageable action steps which make the whole job of doing content writing more manageable.

Now is the time to do some searching on Google to network by joining communities that have similar interests like you, posting on discussion platforms and actively promoting the site to specialist blog directories, Alexa and article directories through linking and backlinking to your blog. Integrating the ADSENSE tool in the site is the key way to earn dollars through clicks, and make sure that the clicks are genuine, and organic because if you cheat by buying click traffic rather than organic traffic raised from your own efforts Google will know and you will be banned by the company. So, now we can move onto the topic of understanding your competitors and this important.

Before, you begin any project you must check out the competition because you need to know what you are against. For Instance, you need to know how their site is designed, it's ranking in the search engines, branding, messaging, audience, products content writing, images, and promotions. By lifting the bonnet of the car and taking a look "under the hood" you can also measure what initiatives they are undertaking by tracking their employment of optimization/testing tags, marketing and media, survey tools and social platforms. Once you begin to mind map the site, this is the time to take a look at your competitors' traffic and audiences and begin to understand how and what they are doing so you can do it better. Checking how long they have been in existence gives away a lot.

By researching your competitor's traffic levels and audiences you can measure the traffic you should be receiving, and your target audience. It is advisable to look at direct competitors and companies outside of your direct category and industry that are considered to be the best.

The is just the first step at competitor analysis but will cover how to uncover estimated blog visitors, audience demographics, analytics, media tagging,

SEM and a first look at keywords bringing in traffic.

Setting up the process

Google Trends is a meter for how many people are looking for a precise term over a period of time. Google Trend Platform is a very user-friendly tool applicable globally whereby detailed statistics can be organized depending upon their categories, geographic location, time span, etc and, it also allows you to evaluate between searches. The platform displays small graphs besides the title that shows you how much attention a topic is attracting or not. Let us look at Google Trend's key features, although you will be familiar with most of them because they have been covered.

- Tells you what keywords are popular.
- Comparison between searches.
- Stay updated with the newest trends.

- Classify your results with respect to images, news or YouTube searches.

Ideas for blogs

Competitor awareness: You can enter your competitor's brand name and see what they are trending. If they are escalating, you can perform a deeper study to assess why and how you can take advantage of their strategies for your own blog.

Past Data: Google has plenty of information you can use for your brand in the future. With the help of past data, you will pick out the most general keywords, a relatively fixed trend. You can then use those keywords while they are on the way to the top to compose and publish your content.

Coming up with keywords: Google Trends also helps you refine your keyword search targeted to a particular locality or region which will help you to decide whether it is profitable to use those keywords in your blog while targeting those locations.

Using Google Trends is easy but figuring out how to implement most of the information takes some time to master. Use Google Trends as a reference source for your digital marketing and content related strategy and keep up with new developments.

Once you have been running your blog for a year or so, try running it through Google Console. You enter your site's domain name and check what's right and what's wrong. Google is in the business of making money and is inspired by its paying clientele to offer quality websites to its consumers, so they regularly surf our sites and recording things that they notice which we need updating to remain top in listings. You may have remarkable keywords, marvelous content, and descriptions in place, lots of quality backlinks, but if your site is not orderly on the technical side, they just won't be seeing you.

The Google Console application is found in the "webmaster directory section of the Google website. You can also find it under the "Google Tools" selection if you are using Chrome as a browser. The first time you will need to open it and copy the "SPF - TXT" record link they will give you and then go to where you have registered your domain and paste it into your.txt record line attached to your domain. Then you will need to go back to the tool and verify your ownership of the domain (button click to finish this step). Once done wait about 24 hours or so to give Google a chance to run its queries against your site so it can start recording for you within your console what your site errors are. With mobile applications being so popular you can check whether your site has been optimized for a responsive design. There could be errors like the font is too small, images are blurred, pages too close and over-lapping using outdated software like Adobe Flash Player.

Once you get familiar with this app, and you must make your blog technically perfect, and your site visitors will escalate. You can hit buttons within the console to say the item was fixed and you can test pages for phone and tablet errors. The device will tell you page by page as to what needs to be revised to satisfy Google's strict criteria for selection in listings page.

Chapter 3: Long Tail Keywords

To bring in the money, your blog should be visible to search engines like Google, Yahoo, etc. Your blog must be easily searchable by Google, therefore is vital to make sure that you are providing a quality filled content to grab that No. 1 spot in the search engine directories. You need to put some thought into the title of your blog. This is where matters can get interesting because it requires some ingenuity to look into niches, your competitors and keyword searches.

A beguiling title can give you a lot of success because that is how your followers and visitors will remember your blog. It can also go the other way and not work for you, that means you need to look again and dig deeper as to how search engine work and rename your blog based. Go ahead and do some more phrase searches if you need to. As the proprietor of your site, your first goal is to be number one when a prospect searches for your topic. The best way to assess the strength of a site's name is by comparing it with other phrases people use to elicit information about the same topic. Write it all down and then work ideas around it until you get the right fit.

What are longtail keywords?

First, of all a keyword is basically anything that you type into a search engine like Google. There are two types of keywords (a) short tail keywords (b) long tail keywords.

A short tail keyword consists of three words or less such as "flights to Prague" and long tail keywords consist of four or more words such as "flights to Prague with accommodation." For the purposes of this ebook, we are going to concentrate largely on long tail keywords because they have a lot less competition. If you write in shorter words into the Google search bar, the results produced can be as many as 85,000 plus. To make your life easier,

Google has something called "Google keyword tool" which is free to use, you go straight to it and look up your long tail keyword, once the results page arrives, click on the first result and look at the statistics.

Look out for some searches made to be around three thousand, anything less holds no appeal. These statistics can vary from day to day, but they will give you an excellent idea of all trends and what people are searching for within your niche.

Now that you have your long tail keyword that is relevant to your site you need to go to your Google search engine and type in your keyword. To get specific results about your blog insert speech marks at the front and end "flights to Prague with accommodation." You are now wondering why? This will tell Google only derive data on the precise keywords that you typed in and not anything else.

Smaller but appropriate

The longtail keyword represents addressing a subniche of your main product so that you're targeting a smaller but more appropriate audience. By doing this, you can increase your scope for repeat business and engage their interest in new products and courses.

This means using more words in your phrase (such as 'free blog traffic for cryptocurrencies' instead of just 'website traffic for investors'), but the number of words is NOT actually related to whether the term is longtail or not. For example, you could offer 'get $50.00 extra in cryptocurrencies' and be targeting a generic audience, or say ' get $50.00 in your bitcoin account now' and be targeting a much more specific group of people.

Blogs are a skillful way of capturing strong longtail keywords, but the success lies in the ploys you use to make some cash for yourself. Blogs posts often a comprehensive variety of topics, which are more practical and consumer orientated, compared to traffic engineered websites. To gain an advantage, employ categories to funnel in organic traffic.

A satisfactory method to get the balance correct is by amalgamating a conscious subject area, as in a broad keyword. Then just as you would with a domain create compacted base of groupings. Then post to your blog with your normal non-SEO, spontaneous style. This will help you earn revenue off your subject, i.e., by posting learning and placing Adsense on the blog. This will enable you to derive good data. Also you can insert Google Analytics on the blog, and statistics packages to facilitate some serious long keyword data capturing. You will find some good ones, and they need to be incorporated into PPC or content marketing.

Chapter 4: Links Are Important

Once you set up your blog and you will look into getting links for it so that you can build your reputation as someone who has a decent blog. Obtaining links from other sites that "like" your blog can do that for you.

That text in search marketing terms is called the 'link keyword phrase.' This means, rather than just adding 'click here' or some random text, it's much more useful to use descriptive text that gives the person looking at the link an idea of what's on the end of it.

When it comes to trying to give the search engines some consideration in this linking effort, search engines really only give you one thing to do - input a word or phrase which they use to conclude which results to display. 'Longtail keyword phrases' is something you should care about because in marketing terms, the word long tail refers to the way to become more defined in your marketing messages, the fewer people it will apply to, but they apply more to those people.

For example, if your blog was about teaching people how to get" freer website traffic" to their blog, you could use the term "web traffic" in your marketing message. Obviously, there are many types of web traffic, like paid, targeted, free and untargeted - so by using an all-purpose term you may be targeting people who are looking for something other than what your blog offers and that is a waste of time. So relevancy is of paramount importance to Google, and the robots scour the website for this.

If instead, you were to use the term "increase your free website traffic," then it is going to make it much more obvious what is on offer and thus be more likely to appeal to those people searching what your blog can offer.

As a blogger, you are free to advertise and sell as many products as you like because the space on the Internet is limitless. Therefore, to correctly market what you have, you need to fine tune more focused message in describing what we have to those people that are seeking exactly what we are promoting. You could end up with more marketing work to do - but it's much more targeted, and you get better results. And remember that with the Internet it is a global market, and these Google is actively promoting this with Google Market Finder.

Google uses links to quantify the influence of your blog pages. The software it uses is called Google's Algorithm, and if the page attracts links from other blogs, it increases the importance of a page. For, e.g. Page B loves Page G. So, basically Page B is voting in favor of Page G and is getting Google's approval because it suits the software's working pattern. However, there is the small matter of the "no follow tag" this tag enables links to be added in a blog's page to create a contactable connection to another blog page and not "liking" them. This will occur mainly in text link adverts where visitors to some other blog page without a vote. You are going to want to have further information on this and looking at on Wikipedia is one way to find out.

Regarding the matter of votes here is how to look at it: In an election, a politician wins when they secure more votes than their opponents, so blogs secure first position in the search engine results by winning over likes from other pages. Whereas with search engines this can vary considerably. The best thing to do is make sure that you only have three or four links to your page that Google will accept, anything more would go against you.

So, now you want to get into the whole argument of how to obtain links that are authoritative? Well, that is easy. Link your blog to something that is reputable and has been on the Internet for many years. There is no point in linking to small and new sites because there is that all elements of trust and age. As you have to put a lot of thought into looking at obtaining the best link, many bloggers resort to link spams, Google hates spammers!

Link spams are the worst way forward, and Google definitely does not like it, and you will get a low position in the search engines. If possible avoid buying links from link building companies because they obtain their data from places like article directories, link farms, forums, blogs, social media, and hubs. So, you are now wondering well what I do to get a perfect hyperlink. The answer is simple a link like that resides on the blog page where the readers are interested and passionate about what they read. They want to read your content and make comments on it. That is why you can understand that it essential not to have bad practices from the very beginning. This element of link building and acceptance by Google is unregulated in establishing a site's authority.

When monetizing your blog, you want to keep in mind that your links should be clean and merit-based. Link spam requires very little effort but then they will be purged by Google, and your site will lose its status within the search engine rankings. Don't let this put you off because it is good practice and if you have the resources and the passion for sticking to these rules, your links will stand the test of time. One of the key elements is the research material you use for your activities. There has been much improvement in the way software detect link spammers it is best not give into cheap and fraudulent link building. You are thinking, is it worth it? Link building should be just that if link building requires no effort, then it's not worth it. It will be the cause of frustrations, and at times you will want to just walk away from your blog in desperation, do that then but always come back to it after a few days and try again.

Internal Link Building

Okay, what is internal link building? There are two parts to this explanation. The first one is that good SEO practice is one of the most authoritative ways that you can impress Google to select you for high page rank. Internal link construction enables a robot to comprehend exactly which pages are important within your blog and what search terms they should be added to their guide of indexes.

The second one is that search robots are just that robots or spider or bots. They are not designed for an intelligence expedition to your blog. They are only intended to accumulate files and compare to what has been given to them by their boss Google, and they have to evaluate on what they discover when searching your blog pages. You can already feel that your site has to give them unambiguous data so that they can take it away and process it.

Internal linking is one way to give those mechanical beasts important information. If your blog is all about selling apps, then your sales page should state that clearly. The phrase you want to use in the search engine is " cool apps for gaming." By developing this further, you can share with the search engines by joining to the phrase "apps for gaming" from any other page to your buying page. That is what the robot is programmed to do, and it will look for just that.

If all the blog pages have that phrase just once and connect back to your closing page, the robot will make the connection "fine, ticks all the boxed" "cool apps for gaming" and they will rank it accordingly. But should you want to rank for more than one keyword. How do you do that?

That is easy you build internal links for some keywords all leading back to the sales page. Remember that build slowly, gradually increase and link up through writing more articles. This way you will get more attention from the robots because they will get used to reading this frequently. To get started to focus on a single phrase or word, and you will see more conclusive outcomes. Once you have established that keyword phrase with the search engine results in you introduce another and do the same and stick to the initial keyword while linking them to the second one. This is not an excuse, but the robots like a fishing boat in heavy waters so they need to have time to digest it all before they apply it to your blog site.

Provided you can keep up the momentum with this skill, your site will get a good reputation that governs almost any niche over the course of time. You can apply as many keywords as you want but the only thing you need to know is that it is subject to the density of your content.

Please do not make the mistake of having too many links on each page. Only populate your pages with 2 or 3 anchor text internal links. Also, don't give in to the temptation of duplicating the link within the same content keep it simple and honest one sales page = to one internal link.

Definition of External Linking

External linking means words in the form of a hyperlink that supports an alternative blog. For example, mypapers.com to another blog called bookreviews.co.uk

This is important for two reasons, and the first is down to high regard because search experts and software developers external links are straightforward to assess as opposed about weighing up and tracking visitors to a blog. The mere fact that the external links have higher visibility makes them easier to log. Visits to a blog are concealed in the blog owner's private servers, and therefore external links are a true and positive way to monitor the attraction of a site.

The other purpose is relevancy. These text links provide useful information about the appropriateness of the blog.

The anchor text that is used in a hyperlink is usually written by a person and is usually reflects the content of the blog page that they are connecting to.

The writing could consist of a short phrase such as ("bestplumbersinOrangeCounty") or the URL of the target page ("bobplumberinSanDiego.com"). These little gems once you get them right, become the target, domains, and source pages provide valuable and what is considered to be appropriate information for the search engine.

Lastly, these types of links tend to highlight relevant content. For example, a plumber's firm in Orange County many have adhesions to the word "plumber." So, when robots examine your site to gauge the status of a blog page. To be successful avoid blogs that are about something else like hairdressing or baking cakes. As we are dealing with robots to do the reading try not to put them off or else it will backfire in your face, and you will lose credibility.

Warning! By allowing your users to post hundreds of links to your blog will quickly put off your users, and make the robots think that you are running a link farm. This could damage the credibility of your blog with serious consequences like penalties by search engines.

If you allow users to make comments on your blog, you need to check them, to make sure that users don't post rubbish comments. A good tip would be to allow visitors is to write their blog address in the comment box, but not within the comment body.

Nothing frustrates a visitor more when they have to view undisclosed paid advertising. They get exasperated when they click on the links and discover advertising and no information. If you go down this route, then source out a way by how you can warn them of it being an advert and if they know this then it's their decision as to how they view this.

When it comes to external links you need to look out for three things:

1. *"Search engines will find my blog for external links."*

2. *"Linking to sites with lower page rank than your website could drop your rating."*

3. *"External links will steal customers away from my blog, and I will lose them."*

Firstly, search engines will only fine if you are linking to disreputable blogs and link farms.

To avoid this, you should avoid any form of mechanized link building. This will take control of your blog away from you. You must always check and see where and what you are linking to.

Search engines want you and your blog to have trustworthy external links to relevant blogs that are similar to yours because these will provide supplementary information about the topic you are going to be publishing.

Secondly, avoid if possible linking to blog sites that are not the best, because it only adds to their status, not yours.

Finally, we will look at networking and building lasting friendships so that you have a steady list of followers. This practice is a conventional way in blogs, and the main social networks uphold their visibility in the search engine results.

Chapter 5: Image Optimization

Once you have put your blog together, the next step is to make it look more interesting by adding images to it. Image SEO or getting your images to rank on Google and other search engines is a good way to get noticed. For this, you need high-quality images that copyright free, and small in size to enable your blog pages to load up quickly.

The speed of loading has a direct connection to the number of bounces you get and your overall revenue, which is about 30 seconds, either way, it impacts your sales. Search engines, consider your loading speed, and the number of bounces you are getting when ranking your site. The reason why so much time has been spent on detailing image optimization because bloggers get carried by the notion of inserting images but there is a certain way to do this, and, because you are making an effort to do everything properly, it is not a good idea to skim this chapter.

You can do many things regarding optimizing your site, your images, and your blog speed. As more and more people are using their smartphones to shop and look for information, it is important to optimize your images as well as your content. Working your way to the top of search engine results can be hard work, but very rewarding in terms of sales and increased organic traffic. So here are the top twelve tips for Image Optimization:

Sensibly Select Images that are Relevant

Remember that most Internet users are more likely to react to the images on your page before they read any text. A thoughtful image will capture attention and inspire readers to investigate and want to share your information. People that are visual often react to emotional stimuli and an appealing image that really connects with your topic is more likely to leave an impression. Take the time and create your own high-quality photos, rather than using royalty free images from the Internet. By using images that show humor or drama with your product means that you are connecting on an emotional level, which is more effective than glossy commercial photos that are technically perfect but rather sterile. Your own photos taken with a good camera are far better for SEO rationales.

Always Use The Highest Quality Format

When you want a search engine to look at your image, they are partial to high-quality content, and high-resolution images. Blog pages that contain images of poor resolution or incorrectly formatted often appear unrecognizable on a mobile screen or a tablet, so you are doing yourself a disservice utilizing low-quality images.

JPEG file formats are best as they provide the smallest file size and best quality.

GIF files good only for thumbnails and decorative images are not for large product images as the file size is very large and they do not crop nicely. PNG files, they can be used for both.

JPEG files and GIF file, because of their diminutive file size excellent for simple decorative images.

Name All Your Images

Now here is the awkward part for good image optimization and a blog page that ranks highly on search engines, it is necessary you do everything possible to support the search engines to select your image.

Search engines bots crawl everything on your page your file names your picture captions so these also must be relevant, descriptive keyword-rich file names.

Simple image descriptions help to raise your profile and enrich the relevance of your content by helping the bots better understand your images.

Alternative text can act as a boost to the captions as they both provide an opportunity to leverage your content for user experience and search optimization.

Name and Optimize Carefully

Alternative attributes are indispensable when a browser cannot correctly extract images it uses alternative elements to recognize images. They are important for adding SEO value to a blog so should include pertinent keywords for the images. Hence, if you look at eBay and Amazon, it is one of the best ways to have your e-commerce products show up on the searches. Keep your descriptions simple and in plain language.

Plan to add model and serial numbers to your alternative attributes so that you don't get into a muddle later on.

Prepare Alternative Attributes Carefully

Do not use over-optimize by cramming in too many keywords and do not use Alternative Attributes for decorative images as you may be reprimanded for over optimization.

When it comes to images make sure that there are no mistakes and avoid inappropriate captions will cause your blog page bounce rate much higher, the bot will signal to Google's search engine that your site is unreliable and affect your rating.

Link Concise and Precise Captions with your Image

People read captions under images more than the text copy itself according to Kiss Metrics. Therefore, this is a missed opportunity if you leave captions blank - you are missing a good opportunity for SEO and Optimisation. Match image relevance and page relevance, it works so much better.

Multiple images are good for better coverage and Optimum Viewing

Constantly arrange your images in categorization and in context, so they flow smoothly, but be aware of your downloading time. Check the result, keep a balance, i.e. a right number of images with the speediest loading times. More images may mean more conversions, but too many can mean slower downloading time and more bounces.

If you selling a product, including multiple angles so the viewer can have a good look, but do not overdo the number of images as they all take up file space and all need to be optimized.

Optimizing Thumbnails

Using thumbnails also need to be optimized, but they need to be used with care and as small a possible as they can have an accumulative impact. They could affect your page loading times. When placing alternative attribute text to thumbnails be sure to use a very different text to those of the main images or the bots are going to get confused moving from one image to another.

Sitemaps

Sitemaps are important because the bots could have a big problem if your images are not listed specifically in your blog page source code because they won't be able to find them. So, to enable the bots to find the images list them in an image sitemap. Use JavaScript or image popups to enhance the viewability or the shopping experience of your blog page, using Google image sitemaps will make it easier for Google to notice you and place you higher in the rankings.

Background Images

Decorative images such as background, images, buttons, fancy borders or anything else added that is not product related, although they can add a certain amount of visual appeal to the blog they use a lot of file space and therefore slow down your page loading time. This can be detrimental to your blog page and site because people will not wait more than 2 seconds before moving on and the quicker, the better.

Content Delivery Networks

Content delivery networks (CDN) are a widespread place to store content, both image and text for your blog. This can have the advantage of solving any branding issues you may have and help to speed up your page loading times. Also, they can also remove your backlinks and placing them on the domain of the content delivery network instead of your site, and this could harm your referral rate. It is very important to emphasize that backlinks are critical for SEO, so you have to weigh the pros and cons on whether using CNDs is really in your best interests or not

Usability Of Your Web pages and Websites

Once everything is loaded up make sure you test your blog pages and images, so they load up seamlessly, giving no trouble to the bots. Also, check for double-ups and over optimization as both are often detrimental to your rating.

The art of image optimization is something that could mean the difference between your online success or failure. Once you have built up the speed and feel that your blog is ready for launch, then go ahead and do so.

Chapter 6: An Overview of Google's Tools

Google Trends is a meter for how many people are looking for a precise term over a period of time. Google Trend Platform is a very user-friendly tool applicable globally whereby detailed statistics can be organized depending upon their categories, geographic location, time span, etc and, it also allows you to evaluate between searches. The platform displays small graphs besides the title that shows you how much attention a topic is attracting or not. Let us look at Google Trend's key features, although you will be familiar with most of them because they have been covered.

- Tells you what keywords are popular
- Comparison between searches
- Stay updated with the newest trends

- Classify your results concerning images information or YouTube searches.

Google Console

Once you have been running your blog for a year or so, try running it through Google Console. You enter your site's domain name and check what's right and what's wrong. Google is passionately enthused by its advertisers to offer good quality blog sites to its regulars. The robots regularly trawl our sites and record things that require revision to maintain a certain standard. You might have killer phrases, impressive articles, and images in place, lots of quality backlinks, but if your site is not 100% on the technical side it will put them off, and then visibility in the search engines will drop.

" Google's Console," installation is found in the directory section of its main site. In the Chrome app, you locate it in "Google Tools" and follow the guidelines to revise your blog site.

Get set up with Google Console and get your site perfect with them to see your viewing numbers escalate rapidly. You can enter data within the console to say the item was fixed and you can test pages for mobile platform errors so you can see what you need to do page by page to get them to an acceptable standard.

Google+ And Traffic

Google+ is a site similar to Facebook, attracted millions of online users from many areas of the world. It doesn't have Facebook and Twitter numbers, but it's something that you can use to boost your traffic.

Google+ to drive traffic to articles

Firstly, get to know Google+ as much as you can because it's relatively new, and being developed all the time. Familiarize yourself with everything and know what's new and figure out how you can use them to generate traffic. Open your account and start using it to drive traffic to some of your already published content.

 Before you begin socializing with other people, make sure that you create a striking profile so you can attract more attention. List down your hobbies, your professional experience, your areas of expertise, the things that you do, the type of movies that you watch, etc. The idea here is to present yourself to one of your prospective clients so they can easily relate to you.

Send out invites to more people within your network. Expand your network and invite as many potential clients because the more connections you foster, the better. Make sure that you invite those who are really active in Google+ so you can maximize your interaction with them.

Now build your trust, authority, and reputation. Remind yourself that your key objective here is not to make a sale but build some kind of bond. So, avoid doing deliberate adverts. What you want to achieve first is to get your prospects to click the link that will take them to your articles. This will happen if they consider you as an expert in your niche.

Concentrate on being known as an authority in your area. Participate in discussions of industry leaders and talk about the most recent issues in your niche. Offer your opinions and ensure that your prospects will be amazed after reading them.

Also, inter-mingle with your prospects while illustrating your in-depth knowledge. Talk about their key issues in detail and provide the best solutions. Provide answers to questions, offer how-to guides to solve problems, spill in trade secrets, and offer expert tips and advice. Once you've proven your reputation in your field, go ahead and insert links on your posts and you can be assured that your followers will be more than happy to click on them.

In this business, you will find that consistency is the key. It's essential that you're always visible in this portal to promote easy recall. Take at least an hour per day checking your account. Catch up on your comment on your friends' status, pictures, and videos. And of course, don't forget to impart valuable information. This could be the start of building a great relationship with them.

Google My Business

Google has produced developed a new gateway designed to rationalize the efficiency of local commercial outlets within a certain area. It is a new solo platform, from which you stream-line Search, Plus and Maps, revising business information across all platforms speedily.

Most people who had been using Plus and or Places will be transferred to the new app. You will see some revised elements and have admittance to new frequencies where you can gain visibility. This negates the need for a novice to take charge of dire convoluted, time-consuming conversion method.

If you have never employed any of these features within Google to market your business, then do it now. Once on the Google My Business page and press "Get on Google" button, enter all new data, and you have constructed a presence on Google.

How to use Google My Business?

In addition to ingenuously updating your business information across several platforms at once, there are other ways you can use the Google My Business dashboard:

• Nurture participation progression on Plus and its' social gateway because it ties in with all of the search engine applications. You communicate with clientele, obtain referrals, structure and, develop better associations.

• Get +1s and progressive reviews. Instigate your clientele to write objective and honest evaluations for a trustworthy accolade. Enhance your branding further because now you can talk about products on all of these applications.

• Tail user participation. Raise statistical information on how people perceive you. Once you ascertain the content that hits the spot with your audience, create more of it to power your visibility and leverage your organic reach.

• Get information on other Google channels. In addition to Maps, Google+ and Search, the My Business dashboard includes information on Google Analytics and YouTube conduits. Analytics is fundamental to looking into how everything is working for you. And, if something

Is not then look for other possibilities.

Through this app, you can easily build and monitor AdWords Express campaigns. Monetary advertising search is integrated into this application. So, you don't have to keep switching from application to application.

If you have a national business, then you can implement volume uploads in one move. This negates the need to employ another person to do the job on your behalf and saves costs.

Value Of Using Google My Business

These are just some of the benefits to business owners, it does save time and, labor. You don't necessarily have to employ any more staff to do all this.

1. It disseminates your organization's information on platforms, like Maps and Search, that is already mobile-optimized. That means anyone searching for a business like yours using a smartphone or tablet can locate the address, obtain directions, or phone you directly from the dashboard. For local

businesses, this mode of visibility is increasingly important.

2. You have a marvelous opportunity to relate with people who matter. Google+ makes it easy to participate with your clientele. Marketing on the Internet is based on who evaluates your business. This is done through review writing about the good and the bad points of the product or service. Follow through to the reviewer with an email just to connect with them and become their friend. People love that sort of thing because it makes them feel important.

3. Actively cultivate your relationship with this app. With Analytics assimilated into it, you'll have quick and easy access to essential tools needed to measure your effectiveness. At the press of a button you can check how many organic visits occurred in seven days? Seeing this in your dashboard will stimulate you to probe deeper, allowing you to look at the problems. Smarten up your presence on this app by adding images,

answering to comments and initiating a dialogue with your followers.

4. Quickly and effortlessly add Pay Per Click to your repertoire of marketing palate. With AdWords Express incorporated into My Business app, you can manage PPC campaigns that balance your other marketing efforts. This will give you a general idea of daily activities, so you can closely link up your sales tactics and achieve your targets.

5. You don't need to be sitting at your computer to do all of this. If you have taken the steps to become mobile friendly, then all is possible from your phone. The My Business application facilitates for you to administer all your corporate activities through your mobile phone or tablet from anywhere.

6. Through this application, you will learn how your customers are finding you. You can see from the number of visitors how many asked for routes to get to your premises.

While progress for Google+ has been reasonable, it is nowhere near its' competitor Facebook. However, it seems that this platform is more favorable when it comes to getting your blog noticed. Google seems to be pushing for more local exposure to help the business make more sales.

Improve Your Local Ranking

If you already have a listing, you will be transferred to this app. If you are not sure to check, simply visit maps.google.com and look for your company. Select the "more info" link, and you will be navigated to your Google+ Local page. You can then customize your details on the profile section.

To raise your local visibility customize Google+ Local page. Just stick to what you know of search engine optimization (SEO), list a phone number with a local area code, enter a consistent address and phone number. It has to match with the details on your blog site. As Google searches become smarter and highly refined, this will help the robots recognize your site as close to anyone searching for you. Should you have nationwide company sites, then you will have to make a page for each state and locality.

Google and Revenue

The search engine has regalia of inventions and technologies, and for some, there is a monetary cost. Google derives a significant amount of revenue from its search engine by selling space on AdWords. That is it's paid advertising program. It has produced a steady income for them Google whereby companies buy advertising space on Google's search engine listings. Clients are limited to be paid by the number of clicks they get from visitors.

Is AdWords A Risk Worth Taking?

At the beginning of your blog set-up avoid it because it could cost you too much. You really need to know what you are doing before you get into this. Make, sure that you have built a secure and solid pipeline of organic traffic before you start to splash out. Companies and people market their activities on Google to push their merchandise and services. It is easy to make a sale if someone goes ahead any buys, but on the other hand, no-one may ever buy, and that is how you lose money. Advertisers get paid according to how many legitimate clicks they receive, and the cost of that depends on paying per click regarding the rate of the keyword or long tail catchphrase that will attract visitors to their text advertisement.

Can You Make Money From Google AdWords?

If you know what you are doing like a webmaster

the definitely. Making money using this tool requires specific knowledge and application skills. Many beginners consider AdWords as a quick and easy way to rake some dollars here and there. This is a complete myth, to do it successfully, you need to spend some time investing in tutoring yourself before you make that transition.

Google News

This platform is an exploration network which amasses news from numerous channels all around the globe and matches up text adverts for viewers to these news items from the listing.

If you can to master all of their exacting requirements then it could result in bringing a sizeable chunk of visitors to your blog. Although what you get is fleeting, it does leave a huge footprint.

Being featured in this network is a solid way to invite extra attention to your blog pages. If your broadcast is successful, as such, it may impress the many webmasters who can rely on you as a dependable news source within your specific field.

Raising Your Visibility In Google News Channel

To be part of this, you are required to enter details for a request to part of the news. Basically, you ask Google to look over the news content in your blog.

Your blog site is going to require some work like the news content pages have to be perpetual. They cannot be moved around the site or even shut down for any reason. A further technical demand is that each of the pages must carry a triple code. 3-digit. Should this be cumbersome for you then add on another section that has a listing specifically for current affairs with a sitemap.

And there is more, additionally, before submitting your request, your blog has to show ninety days' worth of news before submitting your request for inclusion. If you are successful, you still need to submit two pieces of fresh news content every day.

Thirdly, you are required to run a "meet the writers" page on your blog. It should include all of the details regarding writers presently writing news for your news section of the blog. If you can provide the network with three or more writers, then they might accept you.

Chapter 7: Organic Versus Paid Traffic

When you first began blogging, you started off with organic traffic. If you can recall you submitted your site to Google, Bing or Yahoo. Naturally, you did your research and know that with most casual web surfers will peruse the first page and click on the first few sites. These people that are surveying your site have no idea that the sidebar is reserved for paid advertising. Unless you are doing something illegal or managed to get your site banned for the more often they see it there, the more they consider your site to be legitimate.

Having a permanent listing does not promise lots of traffic or even any visitors. This is why when you first launch you have to do more organic search engine optimization because you don't want to have the financial outlay that you would have with pay per click advertising.

As the results get better, you get more ambitious, and you would like a bigger market share of the revenue from Google. So, you write out an article, and it draws a vast amount of organic traffic, and then you have a solid backlink. You have not spent any money, the only thing you have invested in some manual labor, some time and a bit of brain power.

If you submitted your article to the top professional article directories, it will be there till posterity and still bring you some solid leads to make a sale. However, this is not true for PPC, or Google Adwords because once you stop paying for traffic through keyword management, the traffic will cease too.

If you are thinking of purchasing traffic through Google Adwords – PPC (Pay Per Click) keep in mind that because are new to this, and do not have in-depth knowledge, it could cost you a lot and that is something you want to avoid.

In this section, you will get the opportunity to compare the experience of two people who managed to get to No 1 on Google's search engine by using completely different methods. One did it using the paid Google PPC (sponsored results), and the other did it using the free YouTube video marketing and article marketing (organic search results). Both were targeting the same key phrase.

A Tale Of Two Traffickers Seekers

Here is a comparison between the two methods.

The first person did their in-depth keyword research and came up with an exceptional phrase that they wanted. They had money to spend, so they opened an AdSense account, made an advert, and started to run it. They were paying a lot of money to be in the supported results on the top page of Google.

By coincidence, the other person came up with the same phrase. Then they made some different videos, each of which they believed to be likely to become a successful way to draw traffic to their blog. They spent time making one funny and emotionally thrilling video. Then they uploaded all their videos to YouTube, used strong and amusing keyword in the titles, and also made the titles and descriptions very amusing. They enabled user comments and encouraged the viewers to comment on what they had seen and drew traffic to their site.

One of these videos became a big hit with the viewers, and it became extremely visited and commented on. In a very short space of time, this video started to come up on the first page of Google, right next to the paid advert of the other marketer. The difference is that they are commanding a very high position in the highly trusted organic search results, without paying for anything other than the price of producing the video.

Chapter 8: Mobile-Friendly

For, sometimes Google has been fine-tuning their package regarding mobile responsive sites it's now become a part of their algorithm. It is important to make your blog mobile responsive because a lot of people perform searches while they are on the move.

You need to have your blog site properly optimized before Google allows you to enter the search engine rankings.

Google's algorithms

The updated algorithmic software requires that your blog either needs to have a proper sizing, to fit in with Google's algorithms.

This development will affect blog status with the search results. If your blog fails on the technical side for phones and tablets, it will lose its' spot in the final results. The robots are going to have problems reading the site, especially when uploading the pages. If the images are shadowy and hazy, the text appears too small, everything is being squeezed in to fit, then you need to change all of that.

However, this will only impact upon searches conducted on phones and tablets, so rankings based on desktop and laptops should remain steady. If you are not very high in the rankings, then the effect is negligible. Also, by using long tail keywords, you can target a specific group of people who are searching for your kind of product.

However, if wish to rely on search traffic to generate leads for your business, then it might worth updating your main site to be mobile responsive.

To check whether your site is mobile friendly simply search for how friendly is my mobile site and you will get immediate results.

A mobile optimized blog is separate from your main website. So, if someone is mobile and are searching for something then if the site is mobile friendly they will get a mini version of the main blog.

Essentially a blog site that is coded to be 'Responsive' will robotically crop and reduce the content on the page for the finest viewing experience, depending on whether it is a mobile phone or a tablet. And, different sizes are catered for, no-one likes to squint when they are searching, and so it's all part of best practice.

Chapter 9: Marketing Your Own and Affiliate Products

Before you get into any type of partnering, you must have a vision as to what you would lie to get out of it. You have to plan and set targets to achieve anything you want from this venture. Many of us get exasperated, give up and lose it all. Should you want to market your own products then read this chapter and implement the rules set out here.

Look at What Sells

If you want to sell anything at the moment online, then look at the some of the biggest affiliate companies like Amazon, Click Bank. Do you research meticulously because although most programs are free to the seller, they do require a lot of hard work, and dedication.

Decide What You Want Out Of This

What do you want to gain out of this? Maybe you want to change your environment and have a better work and family time balance, or you want a retirement income or just a little extra cash from time to time. Affiliate Marketing is not just some get rich scheme but, it can give you financial stability and some money to live the life you want. If you persevere with your blog, there is a light at the end of the tunnel. Once you have decided that you would like to take the plunge, then bear in mind there are no short-cuts.

Internet Authorities

One of the best paths to making it in affiliate marketing is to become an "expert" in some topic and feel confident about knowing everything you need to know. Once this is done, you can upsell just about anything because your followers have gained your trust. With the odd exception, a lot of them are probably no different than you and I.

Template Websites

Don't go around building blog sites and stuff like that. Do a search on Google for affiliate marketing products, and it will show some of the best ones. Make sure that you research them properly and select one that engages your passion. Template blog sites are easy to customize and manage, once again you have to educate yourself before you take the   plunge. Avoid taking shortcuts and using underhanded methods of gaining clicks and getting your followers to buy from you. Google assess blogs by trust, relevancy, and authority and you get blocked if you are practicing this bad habit. You may not think that this is an important issue, but once your site gets blocked, it is nearly impossible to raise it again.

Traffic and Visitors

One of your key components within this field is going to be traffic and visitors. Basically, you must have gathered by now that this is a learning curve, and practice makes perfect. Take information slowly before you move onto the next step.

Select your subject

Whatever product or service you select make sure that you are comfortable with it and know it thoroughly. It could very well be a hobby like painting a car or cake decorating or knitting. The next step is to source out an affiliate marketplace that works for you. Examine their commission payments, check out some reviews about and whether they are reputable or not.

Your Blog

Once you have decided on your blog, then build one and as shown in this book apply the methods and launch. You may have to spend a little on hosting, but everything else is free. You just have to find ways of learning all the time.

Chapter 10: Amazon Associates

Amazon is probably one of the possibilities to monetize your blog when you first launch. They are giant in the Internet field with high status. Consumers love this website because Amazon has built a good reputation over the years, and have a strong policy to protect buyers from being swindled by disreputable sellers. When it comes to shopping online, Amazon is a leader and growing all the time.

Firstly, you don't need any kind of financial outlay or products to sell on Amazon. You are only required to become an associate, select the merchandise and get on with developing your strategy to launch. With every deal that you bring in, you will get paid a percentage depending on who you affiliate with.

When joining the associate's program, some aspects require your utmost attention.

Amazon vs Google

One of the simplest way of promoting the products is through a blog site. With this, you can drop in a partner hyperlink onto your page. The go ahead and pen some articles and populate with graphics giving detailed descriptions. Channel your data through blog directories, social media networks, and email marketing for lots of exposure.

Becoming an affiliate with Amazon is easy. As an Amazon Associate you simply fill in your details on their website, and you are ready to market. One important thing that you should acquaint yourself with how Amazon operates and how as an affiliate you need to behave. You should by now have a plan to work to. Stick to Amazon's way of affiliate marketing, break any of their rules, and like

Google, you could get banned and your account taken away from you permanently.

When focusing on selecting products to sell deliberately electing something that is your passion. It will be the driving force of any campaign. Many, of these duties, become simpler because the whole process has a routine to it. In endorsing a product, you need to write compelling key selling points and accurate product depictions. Do your best to think of fresh new ideas as far as content marketing is concerned, because people buy on reviews. Treat Amazon like your cushion, sit on it so you can make some dollars without any short-cuts or false reviews.

Amazon does provide tools for Internet marketers too which can help you launch your promotions. Amazon does provide a knowledge base and some applications so you can truly come up with exceptional campaigns on their portal.

Chapter 11: The YouTube Way

YouTube sees around 1 billion users every single month, so posting a video on YouTube almost guarantees that it will be seen as long as you use the right keywords. However, not all videos are equal and if you make it professional enough, coupled with the right keywords your viewing statistics will boost considerably.

Making the Video

First, of all decide on what kind of video should you make? You can make any kind of video but keep in mind that your goal is to get people to watch the complete thing and want to know more afterward. You want them to read the description, press the like button, make some comments, and look for a link and, then leave the YouTube site to come to your own website.

It could be a simple two minute on how to do something. It could be a tutorial on Mac computers. These types of videos are immensely popular on YouTube, and they are ready-made to send traffic to your blog because if you give them almost all of the information that they need with the video and then promise them the rest if they go to your website, this will drive traffic.

Don't make a video to simply promote your business because people aren't going to want to watch it. If you create a problem that you help solve it will make a huge difference. You will need to be creative and make a humorous or awesome video that stirs the emotions and features your business as part of it. That for sure will get you the YouTube views and the add-on traffic to follow.

If you have to go down the DIY route, making a video isn't too difficult to do on your own, and you might find that you have a flair for it. However, there are portals like (Fiverr.com) that have some providers doing video production and quite often if you get a few a quotes from three or four selecting one that suits your needs.

Getting Your Keywords

The next step is getting the keywords that you will use in the title and tag sections of the video.

Try and determine whether anyone is actually searching for the keywords that you've chosen. Obviously, with keywords like 'making money' or 'investing' are probably already taken. And, for this, you need "https://adwords.google.com/Keyword Planner." This is the number one tool that will measure the weight of your keywords.

Now, that isn't going to be the search traffic that that term gets on YouTube, but it will give you an idea as to what is popular when it comes to searching and what is not.

Low-Hanging Fruit

One mannerism is to go for "low-hanging fruit." This means deliberately choose keywords for your videos to get a very specific group of people. And this means go for the longtail keywords to weed out anyone who is not suitable.

The tactics of going for low-hanging fruit is that you'll attract a more targeted audience and get ranked on YouTube easier. If you were to go for a broader term such as "weight loss," it would be near impossible to rank today.

Publishing the Video

Finally, you want upload and publish the video. One of the easiest ways is to publish it directly from your video editing program.

Of course, instead, you could just publish it directly on YouTube. You'll need to export it from the video editing program or uploaded it from your camera. Make sure that you check out YouTube's publishing guidelines like format, file size, etc. Once you have your video uploaded, you can create the title and set your tags. Then, you can go ahead and publish it.

Chapter 12: Social Media – The New Look

Social media is a very new aspect of our businesses that has taken over a sizeable parts of not only our marketing plans but also our personal lives.

Major players battle for distinction and market share by adjusting their business models to provide better returns for their shareholders while attempting to improve the user experience. As these techniques develop, how you use these platforms for your business must undergo some evaluation also.

Social Media ROI

While certain movements are stable subtle variables at play can change many factors all of sudden. Facebook announced changes to its news feed, due to some bad publicity regarding data protection and if that matters to your social media marketing, then you will need to account for that change.

So how do you measure the return on your investment in social media?

When Facebook originally started, it was a free-for-all, but because it became saturated with many people jumping on the marketing wagon, it has become problematic to reach any users organically through their feed.

Most people measure by analyzing engagement. First, lead generation being second place and finalizing a sale being third.

As we all know evaluating a conversion can be very simple or very complex, but for most it comes down to 'are they going to buy from us?' or 'are they just looking?'

What Should Your Business Do?

You can still go ahead and plan for some exposure through social media but just be careful that you are targeting the right audience and interact with them wisely. Do your research thoroughly look at different platforms to gauge how effective it is for your business.

While it may seem tough, it's really not that hard to take a few hours to read up on any recent developments and adjust your efforts accordingly. You really cannot afford to ignore the impact of social media on your Internet activities because you will have competition that you need to address. Try and get ahead of them rather than ignoring what's ahead, because you don't want to fall behind. The Internet is full of free tools that you can use like Google Plus, Instagram, LinkedIn, Facebook and lots more.

Conclusion

Well, there you have it. Now that you've read the book, make the effort to implement all the things that are in it for your benefit. It will take a lot time and effort on your part, but you will get there. Also, if possible try and read this book to gain more insights into making money from blogging. Please leave a review on Amazon!

Blogging for Money

The #1 Complete Guide to Earn $500+ For A Day in 100 Days with High-ROI Facebook Ads and Google AdWords Advertising

Table of Contents

Introduction

The following chapters will discuss the steps that you need to take to use Facebook Advertising and Google Advertising to make a campaign that will bring your blog to the top. Advertising is an important step to ensure that people will see your blog and purchase your product, but no one wants to spend a lot of money and not make anything in return. With the techniques and the steps that we discuss in this guidebook, you will be able to maximize your conversion rate and decrease your costs in no time!

Whether you are trying to become an affiliate marketer, or you have your own products you want to sell on your blog, this guidebook has all the tools that you need to succeed using Facebook Advertising and Google Advertising.

Part 1: An Introduction to Using Facebook Ads and Google AdWords

Chapter 1: AdWords vs. AdSense

The first topic we are going to explore is about the difference between Google AdWords and Google AdSense. Understanding these differences can make it easier to know which option you should go with when you get started on your own campaign. Some of the major differences that happen between these two programs include:

- **AdSense is for website publishers, while AdWords is for businesses.**

The first difference between these two programs is to whom they were designed for. AdWords is more for advertisers while AdSense is more for publishers or website owners. AdWords allows businesses and marketers to use some of the great tools from Google in order to advertise through the Google network. AdSense, on the other hand, will allow publishers to reserve space for AdWords placements on their website.

Now, both of these programs will work together to help Google and their advertising network. Website owners can use AdSense to save space for Google ads, and businesses would be able to use AdWords in order to set budgets and ads to display on the advertising network through Google.

AdSense pays the website owner, businesses pay AdWords

If you are just looking to put some advertisements on your website to monetize it, and you don't have your own personal product to sell, then you would want to work with AdSense. Google will pay you to put up ads of products that are similar to the topic you have on the website. When someone clicks on the link on your website and makes a purchase, then you will get paid.

But, if you are looking to sell your own product through Google, and you are trying to market that product, then you would want to use AdWords. This will allow you to start a campaign through Google and you can pay Google to place your ads on the search and display network.

The setup process can be different.

To get started with each of these programs, you will need separate accounts. To work with

AdWords, you will just spend a few minutes setting up an account and then you are ready to start advertising. You simply need to have a Google account, sign into AdWords with this information, and then choose your preferences for your campaign and you are ready to go.

The process for working with AdSense is going to be a bit different. Google wants to know more about your website and the types of ads that you are willing to display on your page. You will also undergo a review process with Google. They will check your readership, the quality of your website, and more. If you pass the inspection, then you can begin placing advertisements on your website and getting paid for the clicks and impressions that happen from there.

Chapter 2: The Definitions That You Need to Know to Get Started with Google AdWords

Google My Business

Google My Business is an app that is there to help with your business. It is a content sharing, messaging, and email service that you can work through the Google network. Many small and medium businesses will use this to help advertise their services through the local online listing, keep track of their customers, and run custom campaigns to get more sales.

Google Analytics

Google Analytics is a free service offered by Google that provides you with some of the basic analytical tools that you need when working on marketing and SEO. The service is free for anyone to use as long as you have a Google account. Some of the cool features that come with Google Analytics include:

- Tools that look through data that comes through on your campaigns.
- Segmentation to help you analyze your customers.
- Reports that are custom for what you are looking for.
- Email-based sharing and communication
- Works with some other products that are available through Google to make advertising and monitoring your results easier.

AdSense

AdSense is a program that is run by Google. It allows publishers who are in the Google Network and who run their own content sites to serve automatic text, video, image, or interactive media. These advertisements will be handled by Google, but the website publisher is able to earn revenue for posting these advertisements on their website. They can earn this profit through a per-impression or a per-click basis.

Google Network

The Google Network is all the places where any of your ads can appear. This would include placements on mobile phone apps, on websites that partner with Google, and all Google sites. The Google Network is also divided into groups so that you can choose whether you want your ads to show up in one place or another. Some of the groups that you can choose include:

- The Search Network: Google search result pages. It can also show up on other Google sites such as Shopping and Maps as well as other search sites that have partnered up with Google to show ads.

- The Display Network: This would include some other sites like Gmail, Blogger, and YouTube.

The default here is that new ad campaigns are going to be set up to show ads on the whole Google Network. This helps to give your ad maximum exposure to all the people who use Google and their sites. You can always change things if you find that one area is not providing you a good return on investment.

Chapter 3: The Definitions You Need to Know About Facebook Advertising

Facebook Business Manager

Now, we need to take some time to look at the great tools that you can work on Facebook. Facebook Business Manager is a tool that you can use through Facebook in order to allow your business the ability to manage multiple accounts in a secure and easy management. This tool is able to bring together people, advertising accounts, and several pages all at once, without having to click back and forth and hope that you don't get things mixed up.

There are several reasons why you would want to work with Facebook Business Manager, whether your business is large or small. Some of these benefits include:

- A centralized dashboard: Using this tool means that you can access all your Facebook pages without having your personal Facebook account opened. This helps you to separate out your work life and personal life without the distractions. You won't need to log in and out of different accounts because all the pages are in one place. This saves time and can increase your productivity.

- Better control: With this tool, you won't need to be friends with others in order to add them as your page admins with you. You can even control the access of clients and staff by giving them different levels of permission to see the various accounts and pages. And you can revoke these whenever you need.

- Prepare the reports that are needed: This tool can also help you prepare detailed and accurate reports on either a page or a particular post-performance. There are also some customized features that you can use so that it's easier to track the things that are most important to you.

Let's look at placing your first add with Facebook Manager. We will assume that you have already set up your own Facebook Business Manager account here. To do this, use the following steps:

- Go to your dashboard and click Business Manager on the top.
- Go to Create and Manage and then click the Ads Manager before clicking on the Create button.
- There should be a pop-up box, click on Select Guided creation.
- Now, you should be able to pick some important parts of your campaigns. These would include the schedule, the type of ads you want to use, your budget, your target audience, and some campaign objectives.

That is all that you need to do in order to get your first campaign started with Facebook Business Manager. It is simple and easy to use and you can make adjustments to your campaigns as much as you want, and look at your reports to see what is working and what is not working.

Facebook Advertising Accounts

Once your business manager pages are set up, you will want to work on advertising for them and for some of your products. This is where Facebook Advertising Accounts can come in. These accounts make it easy to set up your audience, set your budget, and run the campaigns that you need. You can always have control over these campaigns by watching the reports and making sure that you are getting the conversion rates and the return on investment that you are looking for.

There are a few limits that come with having your Facebook Advertising Account. These are put in place to help protect you. Also, remember that these limits are going to apply to your campaigns and ads that are not deleted. So, if you end up reaching one of these limits, consider going through your old campaigns and deleting some of the ads that are there. Some of the limits that you must watch out for include:

- One user can only have up to 25 ad accounts.
- One of your ad accounts can only have up to 25 users in each account.
- A regular ad account can have a maximum of 5000 ads. If you hit this limit, go through and delete the ones you are no longer using.
- A regular ad account can have a maximum of 1000 sets and 1000 campaigns that aren't deleted.
- An ad account can have up to 50 ads that aren't deleted per ad set.

Chapter 4: Other Definitions That You Should Know

Some of the other definitions that you may need to know to help you with your Facebook Ads and Google AdWords campaign includes:

- PPC: Pay Per Click. These would come with the traditional banner ads. There will be an advertisement with some related content and when a customer decides to click on the ad, you would pay for that. Hopefully, they would also pay for the product that you are offering for sale as well.

- CPV: Cost per view. This is when you are going to pay for each view that you get from customers. With this kind of bidding, you are going to pay for video views or some interactions with your customers, such as a call to action overlays. A view is going to count any time that a customer watches at least 30 seconds of the video, or the whole video if it is shorter than 30 seconds. This works the best if you have more interactive content such as videos for your customers to look at.

- CPC: Cost Per Click. This refers to the amount that you will end up paying for each time someone clicks on one of your marketing campaign. This click is going to represent an interaction between the customer and your product for sale. Every click means that someone was searching or interested in what you are offering.

- CPC bid: This is the amount that you will be willing to pay for the Cost Per Click. Some keywords are popular and will cost more than others. You must take this into consideration when picking out which keywords will work the best for your campaign.

- CPM: Cost per thousand impressions. If you run a large campaign, it is better to go by how much you spend on every thousand customers.

- CPA: Cost per acquisition. This is going to be the amount that you spend for every acquisition that is made through a campaign. To calculate your CPA, you must take the costs you incur and then divide them by conversions.

- Conversion Rate: The conversion rate is the percentage of people who take the action that you desire. If you have a link on your website to sell a product, the conversion rate would be the number of people who click on the link and purchase that product.

- ROI: Return on investment, or ROI, is a performance measure that a company is able to use in order to evaluate how efficient their investment is compared to how efficient other types of investments are. The more money you get from the investment compared to how much you spend on that investment, the higher the return on investment.

Part 2: Getting Started with Facebook Advertising and Google AdWords

Chapter 5: Working with Facebook Advertising

How to choose the right target

Choosing the right target can make a big difference when you are running an advertising campaign on Facebook. You don't want to spend a ton of money on a campaign and then find out you are sending the ad to the wrong people. You need to understand your business and the people who are most likely to purchase your product. When you can do this, it is easier to make sure that you target your ads to the right people.

How to choose profitable images and texts

An image can do so much for your advertisement. You will see that it entices your audience so much more than just having text alone. Having pictures that really sell to your customers can make a big difference in how much profit you will make from your ad campaign.

Picking out pictures doesn't have to be very hard as long as you know what features to look for. If there are people in the picture, make sure that these people are happy and having fun. Picking out the right colors can make a difference. Don't go with ones that have a similar scheme to what is on Facebook, or you will end up getting skipped. A clear and solid value proposition is another method to use in order to attract the eye. Run a contest and have the prize inside the image can be a great way to make it work.

Another option you can choose when adding people into the picture is to add children or animals with your product. These can attract the eye and will get more people to check it out. And in some cases, having a picture that is kind of odd or funny can really stand out on a Facebook feed and get the customers to pay attention to you.

How to create a campaign that is profitable

If you are spending money on a campaign on Facebook, you will want to make sure that the campaign is successful. No business or individual wants to spend thousands of dollars and only make a few hundred dollars for the whole campaign. Learning how to make your campaign successful with Facebook is so important so that you aren't wasting money. Some of the steps that you can take to make sure that your campaign is profitable include:

- Make it interesting: There are millions of people and businesses on Facebook. It is really easy for your advertisement to get lost in all the clutter. Find ways to make it as interesting a possible.

- Make sure that you target properly: You can have the best campaign in the world, but if you target it towards the wrong audience, then it is a big waste of money.

- Use pictures: Pictures are a big eye catcher when it comes to advertising. Long lines of text can be boring. But an attractive picture can really catch the attention of your audience.

- Know how much you have to spend: You need to have a campaign that is big enough for your goals. If you are only willing to spend a small amount in the hopes of a national campaign will get you nowhere. Learn how much is expected for the type of campaign you want to run.

The differences in campaign types

There are two main types of campaigns that you can work on with Facebook Advertising. These include remarketing campaigns and cold traffic campaigns. With a cold traffic campaign, you will work in order to target prospective customers, especially those who may have never heard about your business before. The idea behind working on a cold traffic campaign is to help make more customers aware of what you are selling, to generate some interest in the products you sell, and to help your business build up an audience.

You can also work on remarketing campaigns. Once you have built up an audience and gotten some new customers, you can work on a remarketing campaign with these audiences. These are those who are aware of your brand and your products because of the other campaigns that you did. This is a group of people who maybe already purchased and liked your product, so they will likely to make another purchase.

How to use Facebook Pixel and how it can help.

A Facebook Pixel is a code that you can place on the website. It can help you keep better track of your conversions on Facebook ads, will collect data to help you optimize the ads, builds up some more audience for your future ads, and can help you remarket to qualified leads. It will work by placing and then triggering cookies that track your users as they work to interact with your Facebook ads and your website.

There are several ways that your business is able to collect data from Facebook Pixel tracking so that you can really refine the strategy that you use when advertising on Facebook. Some of the benefits of working with Facebook Pixel include:

- Track conversions: This tool allows you to monitor the way people will interact with your business website after they looked at your ad. You can even look at customers across different apps, so you can see whether people tend to see the ads on their phones, but then switch over to a desktop before they do the purchase, or they could go the other way. This will make it easier to refine your strategy.

- Remarket: This tool will allow you to show ads that are targeted to those who already spent time on your site. You can choose to be really specific with this. For example, you can do an ad to show people the exact product that they left in their cart or that they put on their wish list.

- Create a lookalike audience: Facebook can use targeting data so that you are able to create an audience of those who are very similar in demographics, interests, and likes to those who already interact with your website. This can help you to expand your customer base.

- Run ads that are effective: With Facebook Pixel, your ads are going to be more effective. This is because this tool helps you to improve targeting those who will see the ads and increase the quality of the ads that you run.

You can use the tracking that comes with Facebook Pixel to help you to collect data through two different events. These include standard events that Facebook predefined for you or a custom conversion so you can have more control. When working with the standard events, there are nine options that you can use. You can make things simple by copying and pasting these standard codes. The nine you can choose from include:

- View content
- Search
- Add to cart
- Add to wishlist
- Initiate checkout
- Add payment information
- Make purchase
- Lead
- Complete registration

How to read Facebook metrics

When it comes to Facebook metrics, there are actually a ton of things that you can pay attention to. You will want to make sure you watch the right things, or you could waste a lot of time and money during your campaign. But what statistics should you measure on your Facebook Business page? Some of the best ones to choose include:

- Fan reach: This is simply the numbers of fans on your page that are seeing the posts that you have. This is more of an organic reach, which means that it is only going to show you the views that occurred directly rather than through an act of a fan or a friend. The ones that come from people seeing the post because of a comment, share, or like are known as viral views.

- Organic reach: This is the number of non-fans, fans, and people who have seen your post. With the fan reach, the organic reach will only check the views that are not viral. The difference between this metric and the fan reach above is that with organic reach, you get the views of those who are not fans of the page, but who accessed the page to see the content.

- Engagement: Engagement is going to be the number of people who ended up clicking somewhere on your post. This could include those who clicked on links in the picture, viewed a video, or those who shared and commented on your posts. Engaged users are those who have clicked on your content from anywhere.

- People who talk about your page: This metric is going to be included in the engagement metric. So the number of those who talk about a post will also include those who are engaged in the post. This metric is only going to measure three actions: shares, comments, and likes.

- Click-through rate: CTR is a metric that has been around for a long time. It is there to help you measure the effectiveness of search engine ads, banner advertising, and email marketing. This metric on Facebook is going to let you know the number of people who clicked a link on your content, who looked at a larger version of a picture you posted or watched your video.

- Negative feedback: This would include any actions that a fan takes on one of your pages that would be considered negative. It could be hiding a specific post or hiding future posts from the page, reporting you as spam, or un-liking the page.

Chapter 6: Working with Google AdWords

How to choose the right target

Google AdWords allows you to have control in picking out the right target for your ads. As you work on your blogging website, you should learn more about the types of readers that are already on your site. You can use this information to help you target future readers and customers who would be interested in your blog or website later on. You must make sure that you target your keywords and the ads that you use through this method to make the most out of your advertising budget.

How to choose the right keywords

The right keywords will make a big difference in how many customers you will get. You want to pick out relevant keywords that pertain to your business and what you are selling, while also picking out keywords that will get you the right customers. When a customer types in a keyword or phrase that relates to your product or service, you want them to reach your website.

Google offers a variety of tools that can help you figure out which keywords are going to be the best for your product. You can play around with Google Autocomplete, look through related searches, check out Google Analytics to see what keywords people are using now to find your website and the Keyword Tool so that you can see how often a keyword is being searched for.

There are a number of things that you can do to help narrow down the keywords you want to use. You need to first consider how much you are willing to spend for a keyword. Some keywords are going to cost more than others, so you need to consider your conversion rate to get started to see if one is worth the cost. You should also choose a keyword based on its reach. Expensive keywords will give you a bigger reach because more customers are using them each month, but they can really burn through a budget fast.

You also need to look at the relevance of the keyword. You must consider whether someone who needs your product would actually search for that term or phrase. If the answer is no, then you shouldn't work with that keyword. You can also go with your instinct. This is going to be helpful with your first campaign because you may not have a lot of information to help you figure out what will work.

How to create a campaign that is profitable

Google AdWords is a great tool to use to help your business grow. You can pick the right audience to work with, set your bid, and find customers who are interested in your products. But you need to make sure that you are creating campaigns that will actually bring you in a profit when they are done. Some of the steps that you can do in order to create a successful and profitable Google AdWords campaign include:

- Have a clear goal: Before you get a campaign started, you must make sure that you have your goals in mind. The point of your campaign is to grow sales, rather than just generating more awareness of your brand. You need to know specifically what actions you want to make your market perform before getting started.

- Keep your customer in mind: Create ads that will actually attract your customers.

- Don't mislead the customers at all: All the ads that you create need to be completely accurate for the page that you are advertising. No customer likes to be misled into thinking one thing and then finding out they get something different. Make sure that each group of ads that you are doing is relevant for what you are promoting and that it only shows up for the right queries.

- Use negative keywords: Negative keyword targeting can make a difference. These keywords are related to some of your other keywords that are not exactly related to what is being advertised. This helps to qualify the ads in your campaign and can help make sure that your ads don't show up for users who won't find them relevant.

- Target the ads: Make sure that your targeting strategy has all three options for keyword targeting. These include broad match, phrase match, and exact match. Make your bids for the most exact match keywords and the least broad match.

- Remember your mobile users: There are a lot of your target audiences who will view your ads on their mobile phones. Make sure that you work with ads that are best for mobile in your campaign. This allows you to customize messages and call to actions that work best with mobile phones. This could result in a higher conversion rate and a better experience that is more positive for the customer.

- Always test: You want to plan out various tests to ensure that you are able to maximize your outcome. Don't just be happy with what you get. Try different tests to make sure that you get the best results each time and the best return on investment for your money. Tweak the campaigns as needed.

- Don't forget about the remarketing feature: As long as you have the analytics done properly, you will be able to track the people who visit your website and then figure out who is most likely to convert. You can then get this data back to AdWords so that you can remarket to these people in the hopes of getting them back. This is such a powerful tool that you should use as much as possible because it can really help to increase sales!

Part 3: Practical Applications and Use Cases

Chapter 7: How to Monetize Your Blog

Sell your own products

If you have some of your own products to sell, then turn your blog into a way to sell these products. Don't have a product? You are already a writer for your blog, why not turn that talent and information into an eBook and then sell that through the blog. This is just one of the products you could sell on your blog. You could sell your writing services, an eBook, your cleaning services, or anything else that you can sell.

Monetizing your blog is easy to do after you have accumulated your reader base. You already have the readers there, now it is time to use your own expertise to help sell a product that you want. Just make sure that you showcase the product as a way of helping your customer. If it becomes too salesy and the product doesn't have the best interests of your customers at heart, then you will end up with no sales at all.

Become an affiliate marketer

If you don't have any of your own products to sell, then you still have options. You can become an affiliate marketer and sell products to other companies and individuals. On your blog, you would simply go through and write about a product and say its benefits and features. Then, when someone clicks on your link and makes a purchase, you will earn a little bit of commission on the product.

To make this work, you must pick out good products that your readers will be interested in. If you are a blog about parenting, it won't make a lot of sense to sell products about high-end computers. If you are a cooking blog, you probably don't want to sell products about medication. These may have higher commissions, but if your customers aren't interested in the products, you will never make any money.

The whole point of this is to sell products that your customers actually want. This will entice them to click on the product, and actually purchase the product. You already spent a lot of time working on your blog and making it a reputable site that your readers trust and come check on a regular basis. You want to pick out products that will be highly valuable to the reader. The more clickthrough and conversion you can get from your blog, the more money you can make.

There are a few ways to have these affiliate links. Sometimes, you will write specifically about the product. You could make the blog post kind of 'salesy', or you can write about a topic that is similar to the product, and then add the recommendation in. The second option often provides more value to the customer and can be considered to be more valuable in the search results.

For example, let's say that you are selling a new rake for gardening. It is more effective to write a post that discusses the benefits of gardening to your health, and then recommend the new rake somewhere in the article as a way to make gardening easier.

You can also choose to provide links on the borders of your page. This allows you to advertise a few different products at a time. These links are sometimes harder to get conversions on though since many readers have learned how to ignore them. Also, it is easy to take on too many of these links and it turns your page into a mess very quickly.

Chapter 8: How to Generate Traffic and Sell with Your Blog

You have spent a lot of time working on your blog. You have written some great articles that your readers enjoy and you keep up with it on a regular basis to bring those readers in. Now, it is time to generate some more traffic to the blog so that you can start selling it and make money. This may seem like an uphill battle in the beginning since there are so many other websites and blogs on the internet today. But with a few simple tools, you will be able to generate more traffic to your blog so that you can monetize it today.

SEO

The best method that you can use in order to generate more traffic to your blog is with SEO or search engine optimization. The good news is that there are already a ton of people online out there trying to learn more about services, products, and information that you offer on your blog. The hard part is that you need to figure out the phrases that these people type in when they search for these products. Then, you need to use those keywords and get your site ranked high enough that your website is the one they see during the search.

SEO is great because, when it is done properly, your customers are able to find your website all on their own. And when the customers can do this, they will enter with an open mind about it, and are more likely to make a purchase. When they see an ad for the website, they already know you are selling them something and are less likely to make a purchase. But when they search for your website and find it themselves, they don't feel like they are pressured.

Referrals

Another method to try out is referrals. As long as a referral is positive, it can do wonders for generating more traffic to your website. The easiest ways to get these referrals is to ask for them. If you end up getting a free report or tool to your customers, make sure that you remind them to tell their friends all about it. You can also encourage these referrals with some shortcuts on the bottom of the pages on your site. Then they can choose to click on a button in order to share the information on Facebook or Twitter. In addition, always make sure that you are providing a product that the customer will like. A fantastic product is a surefire way to get the referrals you need.

Forums

There are sure to be some forums online that relate to the topic you discuss on your website. This means that your target audience is already there. You could pick out a few of these forums and then pick out a handle that would identify with your website. You can then interact with these forums, answer questions, talk to others, and more. Make sure to add the link to your website as the signature so that those who are interested will be able to click on it and visit your website.

Working with other blogs

Take some time to find blogs that discuss topics that are close to what you discuss. You also want ones where there are a lot of comments from readers. Then you can go through and start conversations on these websites. Start up conversations with other bloggers, ask questions to the original blogger, or answer questions for other commenters. The more that your name naturally shows up on these blogs, the more people will see your link and be interested in checking them out. This could help you get more of your target audience interested in your site.

Video traffic

We will discuss this more in the next chapter, but you can turn YouTube into your own personal search engine. Just like you write out ten articles about the ten most common questions in your niche, you would do the same thing writing a video for YouTube. You would go through and record a series of short videos, and each one would answer one of these questions. You would then publish them all on YouTube with a link that would go back to your primary authority site.

Chapter 9: How to Generate Traffic and Sell on YouTube

In addition to using Google and Facebook to help advertise your blog and get more sales, you can also use YouTube. This is technically another tool from Google, but it is such a big advantage worth taking a look for it will help you out with your blog. Having high ranking and quality YouTube videos is a great way to make sure that visitors will go and check out your site. Having an official channel on YouTube for your blog is kind of like having a personal video page for your site. You are able to make customizations that let the channel look and feel like your site, but you will end up driving a huge amount of traffic to your website through these videos, in no time.

There are a variety of things that you can do in order to help generate traffic through your YouTube channel. These include:

- Make sure that the content is good. You need to be informative, engaging, and funny to keep your viewers on and watching the whole video. Remember that there are hundreds of thousands of videos on YouTube, what is going to make your video stand out from all the others out there?

- Embed the website and logo into the URL of your video in some way. You can choose to do this with the text at the start or the end of your URL, or include it throughout the video somewhere.

- Have goals for your video: Make sure that they are realistic. There are some videos that can go viral easily and can get millions of views on the first go. But most of the time, this won't happen for you right away. Pick out goals that will help move you forward, but aren't realistic.

- Make the video nice: YouTube has a lot of competition. You aren't going to get far with a video that is hard to hear, hard to look at, and just doesn't look professional. You should take the time to make sure the audio is high quality and that everything comes in clear. Pick out a good camera and editing equipment. If you don't have the experience to do this, hire someone. It will make a difference in the traffic you can get.

- Don't make the video too long: It is fine to make it at least a few minutes, but it's unlikely that you are able to keep your audience interested in the video if it lasts for two hours. Two and a half minutes is about perfect so try to stick with that. Otherwise, people will lose interest and look for something else.

- Ask for some feedback. This is going to help you in a few ways. First, it gives you some ideas on what your customers like and what they don't like so you can make changes in future videos. Plus, if you get a lot of comments on a video, it can help increase your rankings, thus ensuring that more people will see your videos and potentially click on your links and make a purchase.

- Grab your viewers with the right keywords. This is important and should start even with the title. The title of your video can sometimes be more important than the content you post. Having these important keywords in the title is also a great way to boost where you are in search engine results. In addition, adding the word "video" to the title can help you get into more search engine results.

- Embed your videos in as many places as possible. Add it to your blog, to your website, on Digg, Reddit, Twitter, Facebook, and Google Plus. You can also let any email subscribers know when you post a new video. This helps to get the video out to more people who would purchase your product.

- Don't make this an ad. You can work to enhance the video and advertise it to more people, but don't make the whole video an ad. No one wants to sit through that. Get your point across, but do it in a fun and entertaining way. If you can, make a video that relates to your blog or your product, without actually selling something.

- Make videos that people want to share: You want to try to make your video as viral as possible. You can only get so many people through SEO and other means. But if you make a video that people want to share and forward to their friends, this can really increase your reach.

- Stick with your original target audience: This should be the same type of audience that you have for your blog and for the other advertising methods that you use. You want to make sure that you stick with these as much as possible. Branching out too far from the original purpose could make you lose loyal followers, and this can be bad if they are also your customers.

- Watch others in the industry and learn: When you take the time to watch videos that are done by others who are in similar industries as you, it can really help you out.

Watch what they are doing, check out their reviews, and see what you should incorporate or avoid in your videos to be more successful.

Part 4: Getting Your Campaign Started with Facebook Advertising and Google AdWords

Chapter 10: Facebook Advertising Campaigns

Lookalike Audience and when you should use it

A Lookalike audience is a great way to make sure that you are targeting the right customers for your campaign. One of the worst things that you can do is create an amazing campaign and then send it out to the wrong customers. With the Lookalike Audience feature, you are able to make sure that you hit the right target, and that you find the people who are more likely to want your service or product.

With this option, you will show Facebook a list of people who are your page fans, or even your email list. Facebook can then look at the profiles of these individuals, if they can find them, and gather some similar features about them. This can include their age, their demographics, where they live, and some of their hobbies.

Once this feature has this information, it can then search for other profiles that match. You can then target your ad to these people. Since they already match the customers that you currently have, there is a higher likelihood that you will be able to get a good conversion rate and more sales out of it.

Strategies for maximizing conversion rates

Conversion rates are so important when it comes to your ad. If you don't get the customer to do the action that you want, then you will never be able to earn any profits and you will waste a lot of money. Maximizing your conversion rates on Facebook is one of the best ways to ensure that your Facebook ads are successful and you see results. Some of the steps that you can use to make sure that your conversion rates are as high as possible include:

- Target the right way: You can have the best advertisement in the world, but if you don't target properly, then it is a lot of wasted money. Make sure that you do your research to ensure you are targeting the right people.

- Decide what ad type works the best: There are many different types of ads that you can choose, and each industry will see more success with one option over another. The sidebar is a great option and is able to achieve a conversion rate that is five times higher than other options. Some people like to use the right-side ad strategy to help increase brand awareness because they are seen more often. Check out the different options and see which ones align the best with your goals.

- Pick the right timing: If you schedule your ads to come out during lunch time when your customers are working, then you will probably miss out because none of them will see these ads while at work. You can use the Facebook Power Editor in order to pick the specific times and even days for the ad to come out. Sometimes, this will result in a little higher cost if you are going during times and days that are more competitive, but it can help to increase conversion rates.

- Make the ad appealing to the customer: Your customer is hit by a constant stream of advertising. If your advertisement ends up blending into the background, then you are never going to make the sale. Come up with a catchy title, a good picture, and some good copy that will get that ad out into the forefront of your customers' mind.

How to minimize lead cost and maximize your ROI

If you are running a campaign on Facebook, you know that the costs of leads can quickly add up. If each lead were purchasing your product, this wouldn't be a big deal. But this doesn't happen. And if you end up paying without getting many sales, this can quickly get expensive. As an advertiser, you want to learn how to minimize your lead cost as much as possible so that you can increase your return on investing. Let's look at some of the ways that you can do this!

Be relevant

When you work on an ad in Facebook, you are going to receive a relevance score. This is a score that rates you, going from one to ten, and it measures how relevant your ad is to the audience you are targeting. The higher your relevance score, the lower the cost. In addition, the relevance of the ad is going to impact the algorithm of Facebook to display them to the users, and this can end up affecting the cost of your ad.

Relevance can sometimes mean the design of your ad, and other times, it could be the audience you target. Sometimes, a great ad that is designed well can pick the wrong target and this will cost you a higher CPC. Relevant scores can also include other things like negative reviews, click-through rates, clicks, and engagement. The more relevant you are able to make your ad in all these categories, the less your lead cost will be.

Stick with your objective

The objective is going to reflect the goals that you would like to achieve with your ads. Some of the most common goals that you can choose from for this ad will include:

- You would like the ad to reach more of your target audience.
- You would like to get more leads
- You want to end up with more sales
- You want more likes on a page
- You want to get the audience over to your website.

You get to choose the objective, and then Facebook can help you choose the best bidding option from that objective. Of course, you always have the option to change it. If you would like to achieve more leads, for example, then Facebook is going to optimize the ad you have to help accomplish the same.

Build a custom audience

You get the option to choose your audience, so make it as specific as possible. This ensures that you are getting the right people to look at your ad and can increase how many sales you make. You can choose the audience you want to work with based on their interests, their gender, age, or even the country they live in. If you already have a customer email list to work with, you can upload this and then create your own Lookalike audience based on Facebook users who match these people. Or do the same thing with your current fans on Facebook.

The way that you create your audience list is going to have a huge impact on the budget you get for your ads. When you include these different factors, you can easily decrease your click impressions or click per action cost because you are more likely to get people who are actually interested in your products. Take some time on this section so that you are targeting just the people who are most likely to click on your links and make purchases.

Choose the best time to run an ad

You will find that there are actually peak times to showcase your advertising. During some peak times, you may even have to pay more than normal to get your advertisement out there. For example, holidays are peak times where a lot of companies will want to advertise, and this can increase the cost that you pay.

The best way to decrease your costs is to plan ahead of time and always remember some key dates. You can also use Advert Create Tool so that you can still increase your goals, even when the cost for clicks is higher. You can work with ad scheduling to make sure that you don't have ads running at times when you aren't able to follow up on a lead, such as only having it go when the call center is open which can help reduce the cost of running each ad.

When you make sure that you are targeting the right people, that your ad is attractive and will get the attention of your customers, and you pick the best time to reach your customers, then you are sure to get the maximum amount of conversions while keeping the costs that you incur down to a minimum. This effectively provides you with a large return on investment with your Facebook Advertising campaign.

How to do split testing

As an advertiser, split testing is going to be your best friend. The split testing feature from Facebook can help you discover which audience, delivery settings, and ad placements give you the results that you want. Split testing is a way that you can take two advertisements and run them to see which one attracts your customers the most. You can choose different settings such as audience, different fonts, different placements, and more

377

and then use that information to refine the strategy you go with.

Setting up a split test with Facebook is simple. The steps you need to do to set up split testing include:

- Create a new campaign: The first step is to head over to the Ads Manager account and get a new campaign. Go through and decide what your objective is and get things set up the way that you want.

- Choose the variable that you want to test: Remember that you are going to do this with at least two advertisements, so write down which variable you are changing between them. You have three options to choose from with Facebook including Placement, Audience, and Delivery Optimization. There should be differences in the variable between the two tests.

- Set up scheduling and a budget: Scroll down to the Split Test Budget and Schedule section. This is where you are able to insert the amount you want to spend on your test and what times you want the test to run. The default here is that the budget is split 50/50, but you can also change it to a weighted split depending on the ad type you are doing.

If the split testing is done properly, you will be able to use it to learn a lot about your customers. You can find out if there are certain times that work the best for placing the ads if they respond to the right kind of delivery or even if you are working with the right audience.

Mobile ads optimization

Mobile advertising is an important thing when it comes to advertising on Facebook. The majority of your target audience will see your ads on their mobile device because many Facebook users access the site on their phones. If your audience is not able to read your ads because they haven't been optimized for mobile phones, then you are missing out on a ton of people you could sell to.

Facebook knows that many of their customers access them on a mobile platform. This means that there are various methods that you can use in order to create a campaign that works with mobile devices. When you combine this with your regular advertising on mobile devices, you are going to have a powerful campaign that will really bring in the customers.

Too many companies choose to not worry about mobile advertising. They figure that all their customers are going to search for them on a regular desktop. But recent data shows that a huge amount of customers are on their phones doing searches and looking up the information that they need the most. If you don't make sure that your ads are optimized for mobile use, then you are effectively excluding a large portion of your target market.

Chapter 11: Google AdWords Campaign

Lookalike Audience and when would you use it.

Lookalike Audience is a great tool that to use when creating a campaign with Google AdWords. This tool will look at the existing data that you have, including people who visit your website and customer emails and then find some new customers who have some shared interests with your current audience. It is such a powerful tool that you can use to reach your new prospects and it usually is a lot less expensive.

If you are looking to increase your customer base and learn more about the people you are advertising to, this can be a great tool to work with. It can ensure that you are able to find the new customers that you need, ones who will actually be interested in your products, rather than just randomly advertising and hoping you reach the right people. Google AdWords can help you find these customers, simply by looking at your current information. It saves time, it is less expensive than normal advertising, and it can make it easier to get conversions for your product.

Maximizing conversion rate strategies

Conversion rates mean everything when it comes to making money with blogging. If people are visiting your website, but no one is making a purchase, then this is a big waste of money. You want to make sure that you are reaching the right people and staying within your budget. Luckily, there are many strategies you can use to help maximize your conversion rates. Some of the best strategies to work with are:

Remove any keywords that are not converting

You may start out with many different keywords that you want to use on your blog. But it won't take long to see that some are great at converting customers, and others don't do such a great job. Don't keep wasting money on the keywords that aren't providing you the conversions that you need. Instead, cancel those keywords and move your budget over to keywords that do a better job.

Focus on the products that are top converting

If you are working with e-commerce type of products, you want to focus on products that are top converting. You can take a look at the total life of your campaign to see which products are doing well. You want to focus on products that sell best and work more on them to get more conversions.

Rotate your ads

Ad rotation is a neat feature that you can put into place when you accrue a certain number of conversions or you start converting on a regular basis. It helps you do a rotation of several versions of your ad to help you figure out which one is going to work the best for your chosen keywords. You must also make sure that you have your ads set for "Optimize for Conversions" to help you make more sales.

Implement the best converting ad over to some other groups that can use it.

It is a good idea to compare the performance of different ads across the campaign. There always seems to be one that is the killer ad. It is your job to figure out the reasons that this particular ad is doing better than the others. Once you know what the driving factor is, you can compare this to some of the other ads in your campaign and see if they are missing out on this or not. You can add this driving factor to future ads and see if it makes a difference.

How to maximize ROI

If you are working on a campaign with AdWords, you want to make sure that you are getting the best return on investment possible. Some of the ways that you can do this include:

- Adding in search terms
- Use those negative keywords

- The conversion optimizer can help you make sure that you are getting as many conversions as possible with the budget that you set.
- Separation for your ad campaigns. This ensures that you can separate out whatever matters the most for you. Some of the things that you can separate include:
    - Geographical for the campaign level
    - The language
    - Targeting optimization
    - Ad Type
- Pick out an ad schedule that works for your business.

How to minimize your lead cost

Running a campaign with AdWords is a great way to bring in more customers and make more money. But if you don't take the right precautions and use the right steps, it could be expensive.

Learning how to reduce the costs you spend on leads can ensure that you get a great advertising campaign without wasting a lot of money. Some of the steps that you can use to reduce the cost you spend on leads in AdWords include:

Add in some keyword negatives

Many experts advise against working with broad match items because these are expensive and if you do them incorrectly, they can be a big waste of clicks. However, if you are able to use them in the proper way, they may provide you with a ton of targeted keywords that you may not have used. These broad match terms can also help to provide you with a lot of insights on keywords that you would use later on to organically optimize your site.

To find your negative keywords, you simply need to use Google's Keyword Planning Tool. This helps you know what not to rank for on your side. Write down the words that you shouldn't use. Make sure to review your search on a regular basis to help you learn which keywords are the best for you.

Optimize the landing pages

This is an important item to work with, but it is challenging. There are a ton of methods you can use to get leads such as webinars, contact forms, and white papers. But all of these require you to get contact information. So, it is important to send your visitors over to a landing page with a form on it. You want a landing page that is attractive and easy to work with. Never send your customers to a generic service page or homepage.

Some tips that you can use to help optimize your landing page includes:

- Make sure there are some aspects that make a form stand out.
- Keep it brief and to the point.
- If you have them, add in some testimonials.
- If you have a product that is emotional, focus on the benefits.
- If the product is more business or technical, you must focus more on features.
- Don't add links. You don't want your customers going off the page.
- If you sell more than one service or product, make sure you go with different landing pages for each one.
- Your headlines should include some top converting keywords.
- Add in your phone number and use a click-to-call.
- All the copy on the page should be easy to read.
- Add in some logos from any of the big brand clients you have.

- Include any signals that you use for privacy and trust.

When working on your landing page, make sure that the copy matches. If you advertise low rates for your product, but then the customer can't find anything about the costs on the landing page, then you will end up with some frustrated customers. If you are leading the customer to the landing page with some expectations, then you must meet these expectations.

Increase your quality score

According to Google, there are three factors that are going to affect your quality score. These include the experience on the landing page, the relevance of your ads, and the expected clickthrough rate. Some of the things that you can do to make sure that your quality score is as high as possible include:

- Group the keywords that are alike. If your Ad Groups are tightly targeted, it can be easier to include the similar terms in your landing pages and ads.
- Have different groups for keywords that have a low CTR. You might notice that there are some keywords that seem to have a lower clickthrough rate. You can create a different group for these to see if you can improve the CTR.
- Write ad copy that is compelling. When more people click through your information, your quality score goes up.
- Match what you have in the headline of the landing page to your ad copy.
- Create landing pages that aren't a waste of space. Make them high quality.
- Use ad extensions. You can increase the real estate for search results and see if this increases your clickthrough rates.

How to work on A/B testing

Have you ever been working on a website, or some advertising copy, but can't decide which option to go with when you have two choices? A/B testing could be the right option for you to test these out and decide which one you want to go with. A/B testing is not only good for helping out in email campaigns, but you can also use the Google AdWords A/B testing tool to help you learn what really attracts your customers.

The A/B test allows you to test out the most radical ideas, or even some that are easier, in an environment that is low risk. And since this is a type of testing that most companies will not use with AdWords, it is a marketing tool that can ensure you are ahead of the competition.

Let's take a look at how to get started with this kind of testing. First, you must clearly define your goals. The Google AdWords tools will give you the option to change three variables in your test. You can choose between ad groups, keywords, and bids.

Some of the things that you can test out include:

- Bids: Does increasing the bid lead to more conversions and is it enough to be worth the cost? Does bidding more aggressively help you increase traffic quality on your keywords? What if you placed a higher bid on a keyword?
- Keywords: What happens if you decide to target a near-synonym that you are not sure will work? Try switching from long-tail to short-obvious keywords and see if there is a difference. Try using specific keywords instead of the generic ones.
- Ad copy: The way that you write out your copy can make a difference. Calls to action that use "get" can have more power, or

capitalizing the first letter of all your words can make the copy stand out. Try testing this.

Once you know what you want to test out, you can create the test and use Google AdWords to help you run it. Take good notes of what you see here. What is the customer responding to the best? Are you getting more conversions with one option over the other? Is there something else that you can change from here to get even better results?

You can refine your A/B test and make as many changes as you want, testing out groups of potential customers to see what will work. In the end, you should have a much better idea of what works with your customers and what will bring in more sales. This information can translate into a bigger AdWords campaign that you can use towards your customers.

Mobile ads optimization

Mobile advertising is definitely something you shouldn't miss out on. There are some businesses who assume they don't need this part, but with how many searches are being done on mobile devices, (Google reports that up to 50 percent of searches are now done with a mobile device), you are missing out on a huge portion of your customers if you don't focus on mobile advertising. In addition, mobile search traffic is growing over 200 percent each year. This is a huge opportunity you are missing out on if your company isn't using it.

Google AdWords is set up to help optimize your mobile advertising. This doesn't mean that you should give up on traditional forms of advertising. But when you add in some mobile advertising, you can really start to reach your customers where they spend most of their time.

Extra: Final Advice on Running a Successful Campaign

Google Analytics with Google AdWords

Google Analytics is a service that will provide your business with basic tools and statistics that increase your search engine optimization and can be used for a variety of marketing purpose. The service is free to anyone who possesses a Google account. Some of the features that you can enjoy when using Google Analytics include:

- Visualization tools for your data. This includes motion charts, scorecards, and dashboard. All of these will display any changes that occur to your data over time.
- Segmentation: This can help a company to analyze their subsets and find out whether conversions are occurring or not.
- Customer reports

- Email-based sharing and communication
- Easy integration with the other products that Google offers. This includes Website Optimizer, Data Explorer, and AdWords.

For the most part, Google Analytics is great for helping small to medium-sized retail websites. There are some limitations that make it harder for more complex and big businesses to work with, but it is perfect for many other types.

Google Analytics can work well with Google AdWords. With AdWords, you will be able to create an advertising campaign that you want to reach your customers. You can choose how to reach them, whether you want to stay local or go further out, and so much more.

After the AdWords campaign is set up and running, you can then use Google Analytics to see how well it is doing. You can set this up to check out how many people are heading to your website or looking at your local listing, You can use it to see how many people are purchasing your product. And you can use the demographics information and more to help you learn more about your customers for more customized advertising and marketing later on.

Google My Business with Google AdWords

Google My Business is another option that you can use to help increase traffic and sales for your business. You can use this feature to create your own local listing for your business. This works better than just having a regular business listing. With Google My Business, you will also have a lot of extra tools that will put your business over the top. These tools can help you update your listing whenever needed, engage with your customers from any device that you want, and so much all. An added bonus is that this can all be done for free.

There is so much that you can do when working on Google My Business. Some of the options include:

- Keep the local listing information up to date: This ensures that you are able to reach your customers and that they are able to find you when needed. Do you need to add in a new contact number? Do you need to adjust your hours because of the holidays or a slow season? Google My Business can make it easy to get this done.

- Turn your snapshots into sales: You can draw in new customers with some great photos. These can include some of your favorite menu items or pictures of your products. With Google My Business, you can really showcase what is unique about your business with the ability to add as many pictures as you need.

- Build some customer loyalty through conversation: With the help of Google My Business, reviews can stop being a one-way conversation. You will find out right away when a customer leaves you a review, and then you can respond to it which can open up the lines of communication right away.

- Answer questions ahead of time: You can allow your customers to ask questions about your Google My Business listing. You can also save some time by pinning your frequently asked questions and also highlighting some of the answers that customers find the most useful.

Google My Business is a great way to list and promote your business online. If you use all the features that it has to offer, it will become easier for your customers to find you and your business in no time. There are even options that allow you to bring in Google AdWords to really put you on top of search results. With posts and blogs that can be tied into your business listing, anyone who is looking for your business or a business like yours will be able to find you.

Conclusion

Thank you for making it through to the end of *Blogging for Money*, let's hope it was informative and able to provide you with all of the tools you need to achieve your goals whatever they may be.

The next step is to start using some of the steps that we discussed in this guidebook to make more money with your blog. With a combination of campaigns through Facebook, Google, YouTube, and more, you will be able to easily make money from your personal blog!

Finally, if you found this book useful in any way, a review on Amazon is always appreciated!

CPSIA information can be obtained
at www.ICGtesting.com
Printed in the USA
LVHW051211201218
601201LV00017B/1315/P

9 781731 380531